The B&C Discography: 1968 to 1975

Action, Stable, B&C, Charisma, Pegasus, Peg, Mooncrest, People, Dragon, Sussex and Seven Sun

Award Nominated Updated Edition

The B&C Discography: 1968 to 1975

Action, Stable, B&C, Charisma, Pegasus, Peg, Mooncrest, People, Dragon, Sussex and Seven Sun

Mark Jones

TRP The Record Press

Award Nominated Updated Edition

Legal information

The B&C Discography: 1968 to 1975
Mark Jones

Second edition published 2015 by The Record Press
(Originally published 2013 by The Record Press ISBN 13: 978–0–956353–17–7)

The Record Press is an imprint of Bristol Folk Publications
www.bristol–folk.co.uk

ISBN 13: 978–1–909953–37–6

Copyright © Mark Clinton Jones 2015

Jacket design copyright © Mark Clinton Jones 2015
Digital layout, design and realisation by Bristol Folk Publications
Printed and bound by Lulu.com

NOTICE OF RIGHTS
All rights reserved. The right of Mark Clinton Jones to be identified as the Author of this work has been asserted in accordance with the Copyrights, Designs and Patents Act 1988. No part of this book may be reprinted or reproduced or utilised or transmitted in any form or by any means, electronic or mechanical, including photocopy, recording, or any information storage and retrieval system, including the Internet, without permission in writing from the copyright holder.

Contents

- Introduction...1
- B&C Records Ltd. – a short history...3
- Introduction to the discographies..17
  - Label designs...17
  - Pressing companies used by B&C......................................17
  - Sources used in lists..18
  - Release and deletion dates...18
  - Recommended retail price..19
- **Discographies**..20
  - *Action*...20
    - ACLP/ACLS sequence LPs..20
    - ACMP sequence LP..23
    - ACT 4500 sequence 7" singles...23
    - ACT 4600 sequence 7" singles...27
    - ACT 100 sequence 7" singles...29
    - Promotional 7" EP...29
  - *Stable*..30
    - SLP sequence LP...30
    - SLE sequence LPs...30
    - STA sequence 7" single..31
    - Promotional 7" EP...31
  - *B&C and Charisma*..32
    - CAS sequence LPs (B&C and Charisma).........................32
    - BCB sequence LP (B&C)..53
    - BCM sequence LPs (B&C)...53
    - CS/DCS sequence LPs/double LPs (Charisma)...............55
    - CLASS sequence LPs (Charisma).....................................58
    - CADS sequence double LP (Charisma)...........................59
    - TSS sequence double LP (Charisma)...............................60
    - CGS sequence double LPs (Charisma)............................61
    - CB sequence 7" singles (B&C and Charisma).................62
    - Promotional 7" singles (B&C and Charisma)..................74
  - *Pegasus and Peg*..76
    - PEG sequence LPs...76
    - PS sequence LPs..78
    - Tape versions of CAS sequence LPs.................................79
    - PGS sequence 7" singles..79
    - Promotional 7" records..80
  - *Mooncrest*..81
    - CREST sequence LPs..81
    - MOON sequence 7" singles..87
  - *People*..91
    - PLEO sequence LPs...91
    - PLED sequence double LP...95
    - PLE sequence tape–only release......................................96
    - PEO sequence 7" singles..96
    - Promotional 7" EP...98
  - *Dragon*..99
    - DRLS sequence LPs..99
    - DRA sequence 7" singles...100
  - *Sussex*...104
    - LPSX sequence LPs..104
    - LPDX sequence double LP..106
    - SSX sequence 7" singles..106
  - *Seven Sun*..107
    - SSUN sequence 7" singles...107
  - *And finally*...108
    - A last–ditch cross–label tape–only hits package..........108

Of awards and other things – what's happened since the first edition of *The B&C Discography: 1968 to 1975*

The first edition of this book was nominated for the 2014 Association for Recorded Sound Collections Award for Excellence in Historical Recorded Sound Research.

It didn't win – which isn't surprising considering the competition that it was up against (i.e. recent titles by the sort of people whose books sit proudly on my own bookshelves). What surprised me was that the book was nominated at all. It's sort of akin to being nominated for an Oscar when you've only recently taken up acting. You're not going to win – not first go at least – but you start to get a reputation. That's what goes with a nomination. It's not the culmination of things, it's the point at which you have to seriously up the ante. Those that win do so because they don't stand still; and neither shall I.

In the US, discographical studies are taken very seriously indeed. Academics get awarded very large grants to research into the country's indiginous music and it was the fruits of these mostly funded labours that provided the extremely worthy winners. I, on the other hand, pay my own way when it comes to researching and writing these books. I do the best I can, but both time and funds are limited – and doing it on my tod means that, occasionally, doors remain closed that might otherwise have opened up. Basically, you get taken seriously if you have a large wad of money and the name of a prestigious academic institution or funding body to back you up.

Occasionally, my discographies make back their production costs, but mostly they don't. Forget the time taken in research and the cost of all those train trips to library collections up and down the country. That just goes with the territory.

So why do I carry on? Well, habit mostly, but occasionally I get feedback and the sort of encouragement that makes it all worthwhile. Occasionally, as in the case of the ARSC Award nomination, it's visibly confirmed that I'm getting something right and that people in positions of authority have spotted that there's someone out here quietly getting on with doing some good work.

What would make things even better would be to get paid for my discographical research. Come on guys, there must be a place in UK academia for someone with my knowledge (and associated monomania) about the UK music industry way back when. Ah, but would I find it so interesting if it was a job?

Anyway, based on feedback, I've extended and updated the book to include all B&C–related Charisma releases as well as a few nuggets of updated knowledge that have only come to light since – and because – the original book was published. I took the opportunity to zap a few embarrassing typos whilst I was at it too. Enjoy.

The B&C Discography: 1968 to 1975

Introduction

This book had its beginnings in a combination of *The Famous Charisma Discography* and a spin–off article for *Record Collector*. Feedback from both was pleasantly positive, but what surprised me was the number of suggestions that I should follow up with a book on B&C. For a couple of years I avoided the idea on the basis what I knew about B&C was mostly in its relationship with Charisma. However, a trawl through unused research materials reminded me that I'd gathered lots of information on Stable, Pegasus, Peg and Mooncrest so from point of view of discographical content there was more than enough to make a B&C discography viable. It didn't take long to find out that Action, People, Sussex and Seven Sun had also been members of the B&C stable. The decision was made – *The B&C Discography* would be the second book in the '*Light Engine*' sub–series.

For a short while a madness took hold and I considered including Trojan and all related labels – Ackee, Amalgamated, Ashanti, Attack, Big, Big Shot, Blue Cat, Bread, Clandisc, Coxsone, Down Town, Duke, Duke Reid, Dynamic, Explosion, Gayfeet, GG, Grape, Green Door, Harry J, High Note, Horse, Hot Rod, J–Dan, Jackpot, Joe, Moodisc, Pressure Beat, Randy's, Smash, Song Bird, Studio One, Summit, Tabernacle, Techniques, Treasure Isle and Upsetter. Thank goodness that common sense came to the rescue in time.

So this book covers all of B&C's non–reggae labels, as well as Dragon. The Dragon label is the exception that proves the rule and is included because it was a sub-sidiary of Mooncrest rather than Trojan. Charisma's releases are included up to the point at which their association with B&C came to an abrupt end in July 1975. Those that want to know more specifically about Charisma's operations and/or information on subsequent Charisma releases via Phonogram (1975–1983) and Virgin (1983–1988) are pointed toward *The Famous Charisma Discography*, available in paperback and ebook formats.

Meanwhile, one question that crops up again and again is why no pictures? Well, it's all down to copyright and cost. From experience, I know that negotiating to reproduce sleeves can add years to a project and incur silly costs – for example, EMI, which owns Charisma, once tried to charge me £1,000 (plus VAT) to reproduce 15 Wurzels sleeves. Universal/Sanctuary, which owns much of the B&C catalogue, is a much happier company to deal with but the problem is that although they own the labels they don't own much of the music nor much of the associated artwork because B&C's policy was to license records in one–off deals.

If this book included those images to which permission could be given it would be a very 'bitty' selection of sleeves – and the book would be twice the price. Instead, for sleeves and labels try *discogs.com* and the exemplary *45cat.com*. Just think of it as an exercise in blended learning.

Thanks to

Charisma's Gail Colson and Zigzag's Pete Frame for their help with the original Charisma volume, Al Fenn for information on Decameron's lost releases (and not forgetting Johnny Coppin for putting me in touch), Record Collector's Ian Shirley for encouragement; fellow Charisma sleuth hounds, Mike Clayton and Steve Trump for corrections to the Charisma volume, ARSC for the Award nomination and Colin Richardson, head of Charisma/ B&C's International Department, for some great stuff that I couldn't publish about his B&C opposite number's persistent attempts to spend company money on unnecessary foreign jaunts. Well, what's an International Department for is what I say?

The B&C Discography: 1968 to 1975

Island to be part time ventures only. It was Island's success with Millie's *My Boy Lollipop* in March 1964 that enticed Gopthal into the music business full time.

By 1966 Gopthal, Blackwell and Betteridge wanted to complement their current salesmen-based distribution operations by opening a retail outlet, so the first Musicland shop was opened in Willesden Lane, Kilburn[3]. Gopthal worked in the shop whilst Blackwell and Betteridge concentrated on running Island and licensing records from Jamaica. By 1967 there were seven Musicland outlets including a mail order outlet and a market stall. Of Gopthal's original partners, Creasy and Firth became directors of Musicland, whilst Flynn and Parsons became directors of Beat and Commercial.

In 1968 came an unexpected requirement for change. The local council informed Gopthal that 108, Cambridge Road was going to be demolished for road widening. Gopthal and Betteridge somewhat hurriedly set about finding a new base for operations. They chose 12, Neasden Lane, Willesden, NW10, which had previously been used by the mail order company, New Fairway House Ltd. Island and Beat and Commercial moved in and, rather grandly, gave their new home the name 'Music House'. Rob Bell, who worked for Island and, later, Trojan, described Music House thus:

> ... there was a parking area in front of the long rectangular building that held at least eight cars. One walked in through the front door into a reception area which was to the right ... Doreen, [the Receptionist] sat next to a manual switchboard – one of those intriguing artefacts of telephonic days gone by – dexterously switching jack ended cables. To the left of the reception area, but to the centre of the building a corridor ran up the length of the structure, with offices on each side. The first offices were used by Lee Gopthal and his B&C crew, Jim Flynn, Barry Creasy, Allan [sic] Firth and Fred Parsons. The largest space on the left was a storeroom/warehouse for the Musicland operation, and the last door on the right led into the first Island office which was [David Betteridge's]. He had a large table around which sat Jill Grant, and whichever of the three van reps might be in the building ... The door at the top of the corridor led into the general Island office, with telephone sales, accountancy etc. John Leftly, the accountant [also a board member] had an office to the right of the main office, and then another door led past two more accounting offices into the warehouse area behind.[4]

The two companies found working together to be synergistic – Island had a distribution network of vans driven by knowledgeable reps, sales contacts up and down the country plus contacts and contracts with Jamaican producers, whilst B&C, as Beat and Commercial had started to call itself, was expanding its Musicland retail base. Music House was the hub of operations for both the B&C and Island group of companies and the average day sounds somewhat hectic – Rob Bell again:

> ... trucks would be delivering product from Orlake [one of the pressing companies used by Island and B&C], orders would be pulled for the Island reps. for the Musicland stores who ordered very large amounts, and there would be a constant stream of retailers, some easy to deal with, and others beset by endless credit hassles who seemed to be constantly wading through swamps of poverty and adversity in general ... Gopthal would come in with a huge order ... and say he needed them to be ready by 6 o'clock that evening – in 45 minutes time. In the background would be the whirring of the Pitney Bowes postage machine as orders were being franked for a run to the post office in twenty minutes, just in time to catch the mail. These would have been orders that had come in after the Post Office mail van had already called for and collected the bulk of that day's mail orders.

B&C Records Ltd. – a short history

To say that the B&C group of companies is particularly difficult to research has more than a hint of understatement about it. B&C's prime mover, Lee Gopthal, was, over the years, director of – or otherwise had one or more fingers in – a bewildering number of companies, including rivals, and the number of labels owned or marketed by B&C comes in at around the fifty mark. B&C is mostly remembered on the record collecting scene for its affiliations with Trojan and Charisma, but the company was originally set up in association with Island, with which company it retained very close links until 1972, when the jointly–run Trojan label passed solely to B&C. Although this book is not concerned with Trojan and its myriad number of sub–labels, the organisational history would be misleading, not to mention even more confusing, if it did not include Trojan's operations to some extent. Indeed, at the end of the day, B&C and Trojan went down together and, retaining all assets but minus all liabilities, both companies were resurrected together. That's going a bit too far ahead, though – this book is concerned only with events prior to B&C's liquidation in 1975, though subsequent events are covered briefly just to tie up some otherwise loose ends.

A convenient place to begin the story is on board the Ministry of Transport ship, *Empire Windrush*, in 1948. On 21 June of that year the *Empire Windrush* arrived at Tilbury with the first group of Caribbean migrants to the UK on board. Amongst this group was Sikarum Gopthal, who was described as a "Mechanic" on the passenger inventory[1]. His proposed address was ambiguously listed as "East Croydon". Whether he found work as a mechanic is unknown, but by 1952 he was in business as a tailor, working from a shop at 108, Cambridge Road, Kilburn, NW6. In November 1952 Sikarum's thirteen year old son, Leichman, or Lee, as he was known, left Jamaica for the UK and moved into the flat above his father's shop. Not much is known of subsequent years until, when age allowed, he joined a firm of certified accountants and studied toward professional qualifications.

In the early 1960s Sikarum returned to Jamaica by which time Lee had secured a mortgage on 108, Cambridge Road. He sought tenants to help with repayments and the first in was Sonny Roberts. Roberts built the UK's first black–owned recording studio in the basement and released records on his own Planetone and Swan labels. This venture lasted until 1963 and Planetone records from that year included the Cambridge Road address on labels. The next set of tenants would expand the building's musical operations. In May 1962, Island Records relocated from Jamaica to the UK. To begin with the company ran its UK operations from Chris Blackwell's flat at 4, Rutland Gate Mews, SW7 but Island soon needed more space and moved into the ground floor shop at Cambridge Road late in 1962. Blackwell, along with new Island recruit, David Betteridge, was keen for Gopthal to become involved with Island, presumably because of the combination of his Jamaican origin and his knowledge of accountancy practices.

Initially, the trio considered setting up a purely mail order sales channel. However, Gopthal suggested that door–to–door sales would be a better way to sell records to the now well–established West Indian community, so Gopthal and Island advertised for salesmen. By early 1963 Gopthal had put together the team that was to become the core of B&C and its related companies over the next twelve years – namely Jim Flynn, Barry Creasy, Alan Firth and Fred Parsons. In all, sixteen salesmen were run from Gopthal's bedroom. Of the rest of 108, Cambridge Road, all of the rooms were by now let, mostly to Island. The record selling business was formalised with the incorporation of Beat & Commercial Records Ltd. on 19 April 1963[2]. However, Gopthal did not want to give up his accountancy career and considered Beat and Commercial and his involvement with

The B&C Discography: 1968 to 1975

Piles of albums and forty fives were stacked on rolling carts, or sat in piles between the shelves. Deliveries that had come in during the day, but had not yet been put away. New releases often came in and went out so fast it was pointless to shelve them in the appropriate area. Right then, right where they were was the appropriate area. And over all this mayhem boomed the sound of reggae – there was always time to keep the turntables turning. After the big orders had been pulled and collected or delivered, the mail had gone, and Steve or someone took a last trip to one of the big railway stations to ship by Red Star orders to Dave Bloxham or HR Taylor[5], the midlands distributor, a relative calm descended upon Music House.[6]

Based on Island's example and visible success, Gopthal began striking his own deals with Jamaican producers. An advert placed by B&C in the US music trade magazine, *Billboard*, listed its labels as Action, Amalgamated, Blue Cat, Coxsome [sic] and Tabernacle and went on to say, "Our Retail Division Is Musicland" and that there were now, "Fourteen Branches in London and Suburbs"[7].

However, just as Gopthal was throwing himself into the distribution of Jamaican music, Island was in the process of realigning itself with British pop music. Chris Blackwell had recently discovered how much more income could be derived from white groups, such as the Spencer Davis Group, which didn't just sell large numbers of singles, but also sold LPs in large quantities. Jamaican music tended to be single, rather than LP, oriented, hence missing out on the increased income that could be derived from selling the more lucrative LP format. Chris Blackwell later said:

> It was the end of an era and the beginning of a new one ... Up until then I had spent 75 per cent of my time on Jamaican music and only 25 per cent on pop and rock. I realised it was time to reverse that.[8]

So, with the decision to align with white, British music, Island sold most of its subsidiary labels to Gopthal. However, at the same time, Blackwell, at Gopthal's suggestion, resurrected the dormant Trojan label[9], which became a 50/50 venture between Island and B&C. Island decided to use its West Indies Pop (WIP) 7" catalogue sequence specifically for its British pop output, plus the more obviously commercial of the Jamaican releases, whilst the West Indian (WI) sequence releases were switched to Trojan. The original directors of Trojan were, from B&C/Musicland, Gopthal and Alan Firth plus Island's Graham Walker. B&C's Fred Parsons and Jim Flynn (not forgetting Tilly the secretary) completed Trojan's original staff and, later in the year, Island's Rob Bell moved across to Trojan. At some point, Island's Dave Bloxham also moved to Trojan to work with B&C's Clive Crawley on radio promotion – or 'plugging' as it was commonly known.

On the publishing front, B&C Music Ltd. was incorporated just in time for credits to appear on the first new Trojan release (TR 601)[10]. *Billboard*, in a later article on independent UK record companies, stated that B&C Music was run by Lionel Conway at Island Music[11] Of those reggae labels now run by B&C, many of the earlier Coxsone releases from 1967 and Amalgamated releases from early 1968 had been published by Island Music, but once B&C Music was incorporated, this new credit started to appear comprehensively on B&C releases and on Trojan's expanding number of record labels. Lee Gopthal had obviously learned from Island's example of gaining UK publishing rights on Jamaican product and that spreading the load via numerous limited liability companies looked like a good way of ensuring that if one company went down, then there would still be others to provide income. Either that or the whole lot would collapse like a house of cards. But we're looking into the future here.

The B&C Discography: 1968 to 1975

Trojan, along with its subsidiary labels, began to operate in a near monopoly on the reggae front as rival labels went under or were absorbed into the B&C group of companies. The thinking behind the creation of so many label imprints was that there was too much product from various producers to be released purely on Trojan. Therefore, distinct labels were created for different producers, with Trojan often cherry–picking the best of the crop – or at least, cherry–picking those records considered to have more commercial appeal, which may not be quite the same thing.

B&C's first non–Jamaican label was Action, which continued, with one or two gaps in service, until B&C's eventual liquidation in 1975. One oddity is that the Action label was first listed in the aforementioned May 1968 *Billboard* advert because Action's first release did not appear until around September of that year. The label was formed by noted blues authority, John Abbey, who, along with Bob Kilborn, also produced *Blues and Soul* magazine. Action licensed and released American R&B for the majority of its existence, but was resurrected as an 'ethnic' reggae label under the aegis of Webster Shrowder shortly in advance of B&C's liquidation.

Next up on the label front was Stable, which was added to the B&C Group in late 1968 and provided the first home–grown British music for the company. Stable was run by Simon Stable, who wrote the 'Droppings from the Stable' feature in *International Times*. Oddly, in *Billboard*, a regular article on goings–on in London stated that "The independent Action Stable company has changed its name to B and C Records"[12]. This piece of erroneous news was probably down to the recent formation of the B&C Records Ltd. record company as distinct from the Beat and Commercial Records Ltd. record retail company. Meanwhile, Music House expanded to take in the next door garage so as to cope with Island's increasingly successful LP operations.

It should be mentioned that B&C Records Ltd. was not based at Music House but was, for its whole existence, at 37 Soho Square, London W1[13]. Proceedings on the new B&C label were kicked off in May 1969 with a Merrill Moore single, produced by Action's John Abbey in Los Angeles. To begin with, B&C Records Ltd. continued in the Action mould of licensing US music for UK release, though it soon started to achieve something of an identity crisis by releasing soft reggae and contemporary UK pop, rock and folk.

At some point during 1969, Lee Gopthal had a meeting with Tony Stratton Smith, who managed The Nice, The Bonzo Dog Band and Van der Graaf Generator. The reason behind this particular meeting is lost in the mists of time – perhaps it was Musicland business, because Stratton–Smith is known to have been involved in the retail side of the music business during the 1960s. Gopthal knew that Stratton Smith was frustrated with the various record companies to which his artists were signed, so suggested that he start his own record company in partnership with B&C, who would "handle sales and marketing"[14]. Perhaps this was serendipity, because Charisma's Gail Colson points out that Stratton Smith had already been thinking about setting up a record company:

> I cannot for the life of me remember how Tony met up with Lee Gopthal and B&C – but somewhere along the way he did ... we had the name Charisma and the whole idea of starting a record company way before he came on the scene.[15]

The upshot of this was that Stratton Smith wrote to Gopthal on 15th October, 1969, with a letter of intent to enter "... into an agreement with B&C Records Limited to launch a label to be known as, 'CHARISMA RECORDS', Charisma being a Trade Mark of Stratton Smith Music Ltd."[16]

With B&C handling sales and marketing a close working relationship was formed between the companies, which went so far as to include Lee Gopthal as one of Charisma's directors. It also included Charisma sharing B&C's main LP catalogue number sequence (until late 1971) and its single catalogue sequence (until late 1972), which was the cause of much confusion in trade publications. Later on the companies became even closer – literally – when Charisma moved in to B&C's Soho Square address. The two companies were even close to merging at one point, though this did not eventually come about – more of which later.

Meanwhile, the current distribution set up that B&C and Island had with Philips/Phonodisc wasn't working as well as it might on the Trojan and Action fronts. Apart from the few reggae records that made the charts and so achieved mainstream UK sales, the majority of Trojan releases sold within West Indian enclaves, as did the majority of Action's soul material. Philips' distribution services couldn't service these more parochial needs because it was geared to more mainstream national distribution. Island and B&C came to an agreement with Philips to allow localised distribution via Birmingham's Keith Prowse and H.R. Taylor companies. Island's David Betteridge explained, "The Specialization of these two independent distributors will give us a wider and better distribution of our Trojan product ... but Philips and Phonodisc will hold on to a few major Trojan releases."[17] The average sales for a release on Trojan or one of its associated labels was generally between 3,000 and 4,000[18] and many customers only wanted a song whilst it was still 'hot' in the clubs, so getting the records to the right place at the right time was essential, hence the need for more specialised distribution services.

In June 1970, *The London Gazette* included notice of the possible winding up of Musicland Ltd., which started a confusing series of events on B&C's retail side. Musicland Ltd. was not wound up (at this point, at least) but to confuse the issue, Beat & Commercial Records Ltd. changed its name to Musicland Record Stores Ltd. on 29 July, 1970. Presumably it had been confusing having two companies within the group – Beat & Commercial Records Ltd. and B&C Records Ltd. – sharing the same acronym. In 1971, Musicland Ltd. and Musicland Record Stores Ltd. were joined by the Muzik City chain of shops. These were set up specifically to service a black consumer base and specialised, according to contemporary adverts, in reggae and soul plus jazz imports – with "pop" placed very firmly at the bottom of the list. Muzik City's head office was listed in adverts as being in Music House, which must have been getting very crowded by now.

In April 1972, the directors of Musicland Ltd. were listed as Gopthal, Jim Flynn, Fred Parsons, Barry Creasy and Alan Firth along with Island's David Betteridge and Chris Blackwell. By the look of things, Island pulled out of the company soon after this because a report of the sale of the company listed the directors as comprising only Gopthal, Creasy and Firth[19]. Musicland Ltd. was sold to the rival Scene and Heard chain of record shops, which was owned by Syad Ali. The article stated that a new umbrella company would be formed to run both Musicland and Scene and Heard and that the directors of this company would be Gopthal, Ali and Firth. Seemingly to confuse matters even further (if that were possible) during 1972 Music City Ltd., Muzik City Record Shops Ltd. and Trojanland Ltd. were all incorporated and Gopthal was listed on the board of directors for each. Which, if any, of these was formed as the umbrella company for Musicland and Scene and Heard is unknown. Musicland Ltd. was eventually dissolved in 1973 and Musicland Record Stores Ltd. continued until 1977, when it too was dissolved.

Moving back to the B&C label, to try to give contemporary British rock and folk artists signed to B&C a more consistent image, the Pegasus label was formed in 1971. Atomic Rooster, Andy Roberts and Steeleye Span were transferred from B&C to the new imprint and at least two LPs originally earmarked for B&C were given a 'free transfer' to Pegasus instead. However, Pegasus didn't last long under this name. The story goes that an American label threatened legal action unless the label name was changed, which might, if true, explain how the label name was quietly shortened to Peg in 1972. Once

The B&C Discography: 1968 to 1975

Pegasus was started no further B&C LPs were issued on the full price CAS catalogue sequence, which was now used exclusively by Charisma. B&C continued to release singles on the shared CB sequence as well as releasing budget–priced rock 'n' roll revival LPs on its BCM sequence.

Talking of rock 'n' roll revival, there were plans afoot to create a label especially dedicated to this genre, though as a label imprint of Trojan rather than B&C. *Billboard* reported: "It is understood that [Trojan is] contemplating the introduction of a label which will be devoted to rock 'n' roll. Tentative name for the label is Wild Cat."[20] This label did not materialise, perhaps because there was already a Swedish rock 'n' roll label called Wildcat and records in this genre continued to be issued on B&C on both the BCM and CB sequences. The last B&C release on the CB sequence was CB 190, after which the sequence was used purely by Charisma until that label's demise in 1987. At the tail end of 1972, however, both the new Peg label and the old B&C label were discontinued when B&C Records Ltd. metamorphosed from a record label into a marketing company[21].

By late 1972, Island, had already disentangled itself from B&C's retail operations and had ceased to act as distributor for B&C–related record labels[22]. The process of breaking completely with B&C continued in October, when B&C became sole owners of Trojan, and in November, when Island left Music House to move into a new, purpose–built warehouse in Brentford[23]. Lee Gopthal, sensibly, took this opportunity to retrench and started to prune Trojan, both in terms of the number of sub labels and also in terms of artist roster. The plan was that by the end of the year only Horse, Big Shot, Explosion, Green Door and Attack would remain from Trojan's forty or so sub labels[24].

With Island easing itself out of the picture, it looks as though Gopthal quickly started thinking in terms of creating closer ties between B&C and the increasingly successful Charisma label. The first inkling of these plans came in June 1972 with news of the alignment of Charisma's and B&C's various music publishing companies:

> Although the exact details of the B&C merger with Tony Stratton Smith's Charisma label have still to be announced, both companies' music publishing activities have now been joined together under the management of Mike de Haviland [sic], previously Charisma's promotion manager.[25]

Mike de Havilland[26] had set up Mooncrest Music for Charisma in early 1972 and he now took over management of Brewer Music, one of Charisma's publishing companies, plus Trojan Music and B&C Music, which he now ran alongside Mooncrest Music. Mooncrest Music, after this closer alignment with B&C, later gained sub–publishing rights to Rasta Music, Ginlor Music and Lobek Music[27].

Early in 1973 the Mooncrest record label was set up with Lee Gopthal and Tony Stratton Smith as directors. However, with a confusing mishmash of heavy rock[28], bubblegum pop, light reggae and folk–based music, the whole Mooncrest set up, whatever the aims stated below for the label, looked suspiciously like the old B&C label in all but name. *Billboard* presented quite an in–depth feature on the formation of the label:

> Mooncrest, a joint venture label backed by the B&C–Charisma companies, will function as a "quality" pop label, thus broadening the creative base of the two companies' major involvement in the reggae and contemporary fields ... [The label's first releases will be] singles by Nazareth, Python Lee (formerly Python Lee Jackson) with Dana Gillespie as lead singer, and A and A North, 20–year–old Welsh twin brothers, who are produced by songwriter Ronnie Scott. On the same date, two albums will be released – "Razamanaz" by Nazareth and "Sunny days" by the Canadian band Lighthouse. Nazareth is a former B&C act, as is another of

The B&C Discography: 1968 to 1975

Mooncrest's first signings, Welsh singer Ritchie Francis[29]. Also contracted to the new label is eight–year–old Donna Newman from Manchester, who has recently been seen on television's "Midweek" and "Junior Bandbox" programs.[30]

It is just worth noting that the 'Python Lee' single was released under the band name of Libido. The *Billboard* article went on to give a good indication that Mooncrest, even if it was a 50/50 venture between B&C and Charisma, was very much a B&C company in its everyday make up and operations:

> With B&C supplying marketing services, Mooncrest will be run by a management committee comprising, in addition to Gopthal and Stratton Smith, Clive Crawley (label and promotion manager), formerly promotion manager for B&C–Charisma, Mike de Havilland, manager of the Mooncrest publishing subsidiary, and B&C directors, Jim Flynn and Fred Parsons. Hazel Griffiths has been named press officer ... Introduction of Mooncrest follows the development of B&C as a marketing company and the phasing out of the B&C and Peg labels. "The emphasis will be on quality pop singles as a means of breaking albums," commented Stratton Smith.[31]

Not mentioned in *Billboard* at the time – perhaps it was an emergent strategy ... or perhaps not – was that B&C and Peg label material was later to be reissued on Mooncrest:

> B&C Records has now completed the transfer of all product from the now–demised Pegasus label to Mooncrest. When Pegasus folded about a year ago, several titles were deleted and the rest scheduled to move over to Mooncrest.[32]

Mooncrest wasn't the only new label set up by B&C in 1973 – on the soul front, B&C started the People label. Most of the LPs released on People were licensed from the US Groove Merchant label and many singles were sourced from the Soul Dimension and Master Five labels, whilst other records came from labels such as Scepter and Shotgun. At least one LP – by Doris Troy – was recorded specially for People in the UK. Webster Shrowder, who had started with Musicland and was now in charge of Trojan and Action, was put in charge of the label.

People was marketed as a 'black music' label, aligning itself with the current magazine of the same name, but much like B&C's other non–reggae labels there didn't seem to be any unifying strategy and music from straight–ahead soul, through light reggae to jazz–tinged R&B and even open jazz appeared on the label. A tape–only label compilation only managed to highlight the schitzophrenic nature of the label's offerings.

In August 1973, Tony Stratton Smith and Gail Colson left the rest of Charisma's staff at 70, Compton Street and moved in with B&C at 37, Soho Square, though communication problems soon forced the rest of Charisma's staff to follow. Coinciding with this move, B&C, as part of its recent transformation into a marketing company, started the process of getting a sales team on the road by advertising vacancies for sales staff, telephone sales staff, a marketing assistant and a general accounts clerk[33]. In the midst of this recruitment drive, B&C began an ambitious (not to say costly) television marketing campaign for the latest batch of records on Charisma and Mooncrest:

> B&C has launched a Summer Giants campaign involving eight albums which are being featured on television commercials this week and next in the Granada, ATV Midlands, Yorkshire, Tyne–Tees, Southern and Scotland areas. The albums featured are: Clifford T. Ward, Home Thoughts (CAS 1066); Lindisfarne Live

(Class 2); Genesis Live (Class 1); Peter Hamill [sic], Chameleon In The Shadow Of The Night (CAS 1067); Alan Hull, Pipedream (CAS 1069); Capability Brown, Voice (CAS 1068); Nazareth, Razmanaz [sic] (CREST 1) and Music From Free Creek (CADS 101). The commercial uses music from Clifford T. Ward, Nazareth and Alan Hull [and promotion will] be backed up by music press colour advertising, window displays, posters and point of sale material.[34]

It was a couple more months before B&C's new sales recruits were trained up and their baptism by fire was in marketing *Charisma Disturbance*, a budget compilation put together to celebrate Charisma's fourth anniversary in November 1973. News of further collaboration between the B&C and Charisma camps came when *Music Week* reported on the creation of an international promotion department within what was now variously referred to in the music press as "B&C/Charisma", "Charisma/B&C" or any one of several variations thereof:

> An international promotion service department to back up Phonogram's marketing and distribution has been set up by B&C/Charisma Records. The department headed by Colin Richardson, previously with Charisma Artists, will aim at providing Phonogram with promotional material to back up that company's marketing and distribution of B&C and Charisma labels internationally – except for the USA and Canada. The new department is based at 37 Soho Square, London W.1., and Richardson, assisted by Bob Gilbert, previously with B&C sales, will be responsible for the coordination and dispatch of tapes, negatives and label copy.[35]

Although the two companies seemed to be 'cosying up' well, and despite discussions between Lee Gopthal and Tony Stratton Smith about a formal merger, this idea wasn't taken forward. By the tail end of 1973 the idea, probably much to Charisma's later relief, had been dropped with a – possibly erroneous – reason mooted by Stratton Smith to *Music Week*: "We finally decided against it because of administration problems and fears of muddying the waters. Both companies were successful and we didn't want to cramp the other's style."[36] Perhaps, tellingly, Charisma's Colin Richardson had the following to say about the relationship between Charisma and B&C:

> My recollection of Lee Gopthal is sketchy to say the least. I never really took to the guy and couldn't understand what Strat saw in him (other than finance–related) ... the B&C/Charisma relationship always seemed to me to be a bit of an odd pairing and one that was somewhat uneasy on the personnel side. A bit of 'them and us' ... though maybe that was just me.[37]

In spring 1974, a new artists and repertoire position was created within Mooncrest and, again, evidence that the label was more B&C than Charisma can be seen in the fact that the person chosen came from within B&C, which caused some further reshuffling of people and positions:

> Ian Mitchell is to take up a new position as [A&R] co–ordinator for Mooncrest Records after previously working as an accountant for the B&C Record Group. Matthew Williams has been appointed chief accountant to B&C Records, partly as a replacement and partly as a new position. He was previously accountant for Trojan Records.[38]

The B&C Discography: 1968 to 1975

Mitchell soon moved again and in July was appointed managing director of B&C Music. At the same time, Clive Buckle, one of the sales team taken on in 1973, was made southern sales manager[39]

Also in 1974, B&C looked to further widen its share of the UK soul music market. This time, however, instead of licensing music from myriad labels as they did with Action and People, B&C set up to distribute product from the US Sussex label under that label's own imprint. Of the deal between B&C and Sussex, *Billboard* included brief details:

> B&C Records have completed a deal with U.S. label Sussex, previously with A&M Records for the U.K. First release is a batch of four Bill Withers' albums, and singles from Creative Source, Soul Searchers and Master Fleet. Deal was set up by B&C managing director Lee Gopthal and Sussex president Clarence Avant.[40]

The Sussex label remains a bit of an oddity in that the majority of the LPs issued by B&C still seemed to be available via A&M, their previous UK label. After B&C's demise, these albums were *still* listed in trade publications as being available from A&M. In an odd quirk of fate, perhaps, Sussex did not outlast B&C: Sussex's owner, Clarence Avant was raided and prosecuted by the US Internal Revenue Service for tax evasion, and the label closed in July 1975[41].

Meanwhile, to go back a bit, B&C, as already mentioned, seems to have moved people around the organisation with some regularity, and in October 1974, Steve Jukes, who had recently been put in charge of the Sussex label, took part in what looks suspiciously like a spot of job enlargement:

> As part of the restructuring and strengthening of its promotion activities the B&C/Charisma Group has created the new post of head of promotions. Steve Jukes who was recently appointed manager of the newly signed Sussex label will become head of the promotion department and Fraser Kennedy, who was previously area promotion manager for Scotland and the North East becomes field promotions manager. Changes have also been announced in the structure of the Mooncrest publishing company, which will now be jointly managed by Stephen Shane and Ian Warner ...[42]

Perhaps there were warning bells at Charisma that not all was well within the B&C group of companies. It might otherwise seem odd that, just as B&C was starting to expand, Stratton Smith started to think in terms of distancing Charisma from B&C. Toward the end of 1974 Stratton Smith is documented (admittedly in his own words and after B&C's subsequent liquidation) as having decided that it would be in Charisma's interests to curtail the long–term licensing deal with B&C:

> ... Stratton–Smith explained that he had made his intentions clear at Christmas that he would terminate Charisma's licensing deal with B&C as soon as alternative arrangements could be made. "A licensing deal was too limiting to allow Charisma to develop as I wanted,["] he said. Originally the deal with Phonogram had been planned to start in June but at B&C's request he had agreed to a three–month extension for catalogue sales "to give the company an opportunity to replace the lost business or to gear down to a reduced turnover."[43]

Ironically, it was success that brought about the end of B&C. Ken Boothe's rendition of Bread's *Everything I Own* was a major hit in the UK for Trojan in autumn 1974. B&C used Saga's pressing plant, perhaps because other manufacturers were starting to make noises about extended credit and monies owed them. Whatever the reason, as it turned out Trojan had difficulty in paying Saga the £20,000 pressing costs. Lee Gopthal had perhaps forgotten Island's strategy, in the mid–1960s, of licencing records that they expected to be big hits via a major label: Chris Blackwell, talking about this had said: "I'd seen independent labels die because they had a hit ... They'd run up a huge bill manufacturing the records and then they would have difficulty getting paid on time by retailers and they'd go bankrupt."[44] Perhaps Gopthal genuinely didn't realise that a company as large as B&C could be brought low by something as simple as cash flow problems. That or the size of the hit came as a complete surprise to the company.

Saga's owner, Marcel Rodd, was looking to expand and in March 1975, Saga advertised in *Music Week* to buy a record company as a going concern[45]. B&C, with its seemingly successful Mooncrest and Trojan labels and industry–rumoured cash flow problems, could easily fit the bill. What actually happened, whilst not illegal, remains perhaps morally questionable. Still, as they say, all's fair in business. Well, you've got to say something.

> ... [Saga's accountant, Bill] Ross telephoned B&C/Trojan [who] weren't prepared to sell but an agreement emerged between Rodd and B&C/Trojan's directors Lee Gopthal and Brian Gibbon[46] where, for a 10 per cent interest in the company, Saga would loan B&C [£150,000] to be secured on audited figures showing [£600,000] of net assets. The debenture was drawn up by Saga's solicitors. But meanwhile Bill Ross had spent a week in B&C/Trojan's accounts departments and brought back the alarming news that the contract would have to be scrapped, as in his opinion, the company was "grossly in deficit" ... B&C/Trojan came back to Saga to say that provided Saga could conclude a deal within forty–eight hours they would sell the whole of the company for any figure, "provided it was not less than twenty–five–thousand pounds" ... That's when Saga ... proposed the formation of new subsidiary companies, B&C Recordings Ltd and Trojan Recordings Ltd (with the board of directors identical to B&C Records Ltd and Trojan Records Ltd) and that on formation the new companies should have transferred to them the assets of the parent companies (the stock, recording contracts and masters) but not the liabilities (the growing mountain of unpaid bills) and that the new subsidiaries should then be immediately sold to Saga ... On the 31st May 1975, Saga handed over a cheque for just under [£30,000] to B&C/Trojan. But [instead] of using the cash to try and refloat their floundering company B&C/Trojan merely extinguished their bank overdraft ... then dismissed all their staff and applied to be put into voluntary liquidation.[47]

Notices of two creditors meetings, one for B&C Records Ltd. and one for Trojan Records Ltd., were posted in *The London Gazette* on 10th June, 1975[48]. These meetings were to take place at the Westbury Hotel, New Bond Street, Piccadilly, on 20th June, 1975, at 2.00 pm (for B&C) and 3.30 pm (for Trojan). A further pair of notices was placed in the same paper on 19th June regarding petitions brought by MCPS for the winding up of B&C and Trojan in the High Court of Chancery. The hearing was set for 7th July.

Goings on at B&C, in relation to Charisma's somewhat rushed deal with Phonogram, made the front page of *Music Week* but quite a lot was left unsaid:

> Charisma Records has signed a pressing and distribution deal with Phonogram for the UK and Eire. The pact coincides with news that B&C, which previously handled sales and distribution for Charisma is part of a takeover deal by Saga Records' parent company, Art and Sound Ltd (Saga Sound) ... All B&C employees,

including those at the affiliated Trojan and Mooncrest publishing and recording companies, were given formal notice last Friday (Jun 6) but a rider clause said that some jobs would be saved by the Saga takeover. An announcement from Saga states: "Saga has purchased 100 percent of the shareholdings of B&C Recordings Ltd and Trojan Recordings Ltd, previously known as B&C Records and Trojan Records. Also included in this deal until August 31, this year, are our pressing rights to Charisma Records and thereafter unlimited selling rights on Charisma stocks on hand."[49]

It was a couple more weeks after the original news of the Saga takeover before *Music Week* announced B&C's liquidation, out of which several companies seem to have come out rather badly:

The total estimated deficiency of Trojan Records and B&C Records, 300 people at a creditors' meeting at the Hanover Grand last Friday, were told, amounted to £594,453, with B&C accounting for £408,991 of the full amount. A statement of affairs relating to B&C showed book value assets of £355,972, of which £140,000 related to advance royalties, to an estimated realisable value of £116,000. MCPS with £31,350 was at the top of the schedule of copyright creditors, followed by Carlin Music/Genesis (£23,665), Mooncrest Music (£17,094), Quarter (£14,795), B&C Music (£11,625) and Mountain/Carlin (£9,562). Among the unsecured creditors were Garrod and Lofthouse (£27,476), J. Upton (£24,243), E. J. Day (£11,263), CBS Manufacturing (£16,133), CRS (£11,473), National Publicity (£10,785) and Morgan Studios (£10,000). The total amounted to £316,932.26.[50]

In July 1975, Charisma moved out of 37, Soho Square and retrenched drastically to survive – further information is included in the sister publication, *The Famous Charisma Discography*. Once the crisis was over, Charisma expanded its staff base and brought in several ex–B&C staff, including Clive Crawley. Webster Shrowder, the managing director of Trojan and head of the People and Action labels, was taken on by Saga but left to form Vulcan Records along with Junior Lincoln[51], who had run a resurrected version of the Ashanti label for B&C. Under Saga's ownership, the B&C, Mooncrest and Trojan labels were reactivated, and still exist today, though now several changes of ownership later.

Lee Gopthal, Webster Shrowder, Joe Sinclair and Desmond Bryan were listed as directors of Muzik City Record Shops Ltd. as at 1975, but on 22nd January, 1976, the company went into voluntary winding up, with things dragging on until the final creditors' meeting on 1st December, 1978[52]. It is unclear whether Gopthal was still involved to any extent with Musicland Record Stores Ltd., but this company too was dissolved on 14th February, 1977[53]. Lee Gopthal, following a certain amount of silence, was next reported in the trade press as head of A&R for RCA UK[54]. After this, he moved away from the music industry and went into commerce, type unspecified. He died on 29 August 1997.

Tony Stratton Smith spoke to *Music Week*[55] saying that the reason behind B&C's demise was that they had introduced a sales force despite not having a large enough product base to make this sales expansion viable. Added to this, he said, was a bad sales performance in the first three months of 1975. However, perhaps B&C's demise was due to more deep–seated reasons. Neither B&C nor Trojan, unlike Charisma, were particularly concerned with artist development, probably because the business model was that of licensing existing product from various sources. Consequently, the emphasis tended to be on singles and budget compilation LPs rather than on more lucrative full price album sales. By focusing on singles and budget albums, margin on a per unit basis would never be anything but fairly low. Charisma survived where B&C failed because Stratton Smith was interested, first and foremost, in signing artists whose careers he could develop. More importantly, he concentrated on 'album artists'. Hit singles were lucrative in the short term but worked best as promotional tools for albums. The only sustained success that B&C had with full price album product was with Mooncrest – but Mooncrest's best-selling albums were licensed from production companies, such as Mountain and Sandy Roberton's September Productions[56]. The last word sits with Rob Bell and, as last words go, it speaks volumes about B&C:

> There was no quality control at all, really. I don't think ... Lee [Gopthal] had a huge amount of artistic appreciation. The majority of the folks involved saw the whole thing merely as a business, which of course it was.[57]

The B&C Discography: 1968 to 1975

Section sources

1. Public Record Office Catalogue Reference PRO/BT26/1237/9410. Accessed from http://www.movinghere.org.uk/deliveryfiles/PRO/BT26_1237_9410/0/1.pdf (05/08/2012).
2. According to De Konigh, M. & Cane–Honeycott, L. (in *Young Gifted and Black*, 2003, Sanctuary, p. 29) Beat and Commercial Records Ltd. was set up by Lee Gopthal and Tony Stratton Smith. This is perfectly possible but, if so, it is odd that Stratton Smith's name does not crop up again in official documentation until 1969.
3. De Konigh, M. & Cane–Honeycott, L. (in *Young Gifted and Black*, 2003, Sanctuary, p. 42) note that there is anecdotal evidence of a branch of Musicland existing as early as 1965, but could find no corroborative documentary evidence.
4. Bell, R. (25/03/2009) *Joy, Tears & Endless Kicks – My Life In Music, Part 4*. Accessed from: http://www.sequelmusic.com/index.php?11=1&articleID=158&page= (10/03/2012).
5. HR Taylor did not start distributing Trojan until around June 1970: the original article also mentions the Muzik City chain of record shops, which were started in 1971, so this quote includes various memories spanning 1968 to 1971.
6. Bell, R. (30/03/2009) *Joy, Tears & Endless Kicks – My Life In Music, Part 5*. Accessed from: http://www.sequelmusic.com/index.php?11=1&articleID=301&page= (10/03/2012).
7. Advert (12/05/1968) Spotlight On London. *Billboard*.
8. Blackwell, C., quoted in *Island History* (no author or publication date attributed). Accessed from: http://www.islandrecords.co.uk/history.php (09/04/2012)
9. Trojan was originally set up in 1967 as an Island subsidiary label, but became dormant in early 1968 after the release of TR 015. The B&C/Island joint venture started later in 1968 with TR 600.
10. B&C was also, to a currently unknown extent, associated with Libra Music and Pinewalk Music.
11. No author attributed (13/11/1971) Spotlight On London: The Vigorous, Resourceful Independents. *Billboard*.
12. Palmer, P. (12/04/1969) International New Reports: London. *Billboard*.
13. As regards addresses, the first fifteen or so Island singles included a 4, Rutland Gate Mews, SW7 address. After a few months with no address listed, both singles and LPs, including Island's highly successful series of risqué LPs on the Surprise label, included the 108 Cambridge Road address. By 1968 Island started to use a rather more upmarket 155–157 Oxford Street address on LP sleeves. Action label LPs (and the various reggae labels) used the Music House address – ACLP 6004 includes the following: "A member of B & C Group Music House 12 Neasden Lane London Tel 01 – 459 5222." All B&C, Charisma and Mooncrest LPs included the 37 Soho Square address.
14. No author attributed (17/11/1973) Charisma – artist's label, *Music Week*.
15. Email dated 13th November 2009.
16. Photograph of letter included in the booklet accompanying *The Famous Charisma Box* 4–CD set (CASBOX 1, 1993).
17. No author attributed (13/06/1970) International News Reports: Island Distrib Tie on Trojan, *Billboard*.
18. No author attributed (13/11/1971) Spotlight On London: West Indian Population Sparks New UK Music Trend, *Billboard*.
19. Palaree, P. (20/05/1972) International News Reports: From The Music Capitals of the World: London, *Billboard*.
20. No author attributed (27/03/1971) International News Reports: From The Music Capitals of the World: Reggae Outlet Forms Label, *Billboard*.
21. Notice of release of B&C label 8–tracks and cassettes (of previously–released BCM series LPs) was still being documented in trade publications as late as February 1973, which smacks somewhat of B&C acting as a record label very shortly in advance of its supposed successor, Mooncrest, being launched. It's difficult to disentangle and one gets the distinct impression that B&C was making it up as it went along and claiming some sort of strategy after the event when talking to the press.
22. EMI had taken over from Island/Philips/Phondisc, though EMI would later set up joint distribution with Island and all B&C–related product was listed in trade publications from around mid–1973 as being distributed by Island/EMI.
23. No author attributed (28/10/1972) International News Reports: Island, B&C Split With Trojan Label, *Billboard*.
24. These labels were later augmented, however. In 1973 B&C/Trojan started a new version of the Ashanti label, run by Junior Lincoln. Lincoln had previously run Ashanti as a sub–label of his own Bamboo label, which had been a rival to Trojan until Bamboo went bust. In 1974 Mooncrest (rather than Trojan) picked up the licence for the Dragon label from Island – labels included the text, "Manufactured by Mooncrest Records Ltd", though this was later changed to the more usual, "Marketed by B&C Records".

The B&C Discography: 1968 to 1975

25. Palmer, P. (29/07/1972) International News Reports: From The Music Capitals of the World: London, *Billboard*.
26. Mike de Havilland (correct spelling) had recently changed his name from Mike Paice.
27. No author attributed (01/12/1973) Mooncrest sub–deal, *Music Week*.
28. Mooncrest was referred to as a "heavy rock" label in Japan: see Eguchi, H. (08/09/1973) International News: From the Music Capitals of the World: Tokyo, *Billboard*. The article also referred to the label having been set up in May 1972, which presumably relates to the setting up of the Mooncrest Music publishing company and not the record label. It is comforting to know that, even at the time, journalists had difficulty keeping up with B&C-related companies.
29. A and A North had also previously been signed to B&C, whilst Richie Francis had been signed to Pegasus.
30. No author attributed (10/03/1973) International News Reports: B&C–Charisma Label Widens Cos' Base, *Billboard*.
31. Ibid.
32. Bromeu, J. (01/06/1974) International News: From the Music Capitals of the World: London, *Billboard*.
33. No author attributed (11/08/1973) Advert, *Music Week*.
34. No author attributed (08/09/1973) B&C plans 'Summer' tele–push, *Music Week*.
35. No author attributed (01/09/1973) B&C–Charisma set up promo dept, *Music Week*.
36. No author attributed (17/11/1973) Charisma – artist's label, *Music Week*.
37. Email dated 11/03/2012.
38. No author attributed (20/04/1974) International: International Turntable, *Billboard*.
39. No author attributed (27/07/1974) International: International Turntable, *Billboard*.
40. Jones, P. (29/09/1974) International: From the Music Capitals of the World: London, *Billboard*.
41. After its offices were padlocked by the IRS.
42. White, C. (05/10/1974) International News: From the Music Capitals of the World: London, *Billboard*.
43. No author attributed (05/07/1975) Charisma surges back with new talent push, *Music Week*.
44. Blackwell, C., quoted in *Island History* (no author or publication date attributed). Accessed from: http://www.islandrecords.co.uk/history.php (09/04/2012)
45. No author attributed (10/1976) Reggae Business, *Black Music Magazine*. p23
46. Brian Gibbon almost immediately joined Charisma as deputy managing director. Or was already working for both B&C and Charisma.
47. No author attributed (10/1976) Reggae Business, *Black Music Magazine*. pp23–4
48. De Koningh, M. & Cane–Honeycott, L. (2003) *Young Gifted and Black*. Sanctuary, p. 76.
49. Jones, P. (14/06/1975) Charisma to Phonogram as Saga acquires B&C, *Music Week*.
50. No author attributed (28/06/1975) Trojan–B&C liquidation, *Music Week*.
51. No author attributed (13/09/1975) International: Trojan Execs Form a label, *Billboard*. The company was originally going to be called Viking Records and is named as such in this article.
52. De Koningh, M. & Cane–Honeycott, L. (2003) *Young Gifted and Black*. Sanctuary, pp. 30–31.
53. Ibid.
54. Jones, P. (25/12/1976) International: From The Music Capitals of the World: London, *Billboard*.
55. No author attributed (05/07/1975) Charisma surges back with new talent push, *Music Week*.
56. Sadly, for Saga, both license deals had come to an end immediately prior to Saga acquiring Mooncrest. Mountain quickly turned itself into a record label, with distribution by Phonogram, and successfully reissued the entire Nazareth album back catalogue. Sandy Roberton continued to license his records to the resurrected Mooncrest.
57. De Koningh, M. & Cane–Honeysett, L. (2003) *Young Gifted and Black*. Sanctuary, p. 47.

Michael de Koningh and Laurence Cane–Honeysett's *Young Gifted and Black: The Story of Trojan Records* (Sanctuary, 2003) is highly recommended for further information on Lee Gopthal and B&C. Although focused on the Trojan series of labels it provides a great deal of contextualisation of material in the organisational history in this discography.

Introduction to the discographies

Label designs

The listings only include original label design information where one or more records in a particular catalogue sequence appeared on more than one design. Records on Stable, Mooncrest, Sussex, People and Seven Sun only appeared on one label design, as did LPs on Action's ACLP/ACLS sequence, so label information is not required for these.

7" label designs	LP label designs
AC1 – Action: orange and yellow	BC1 – B&C: black with silver logo
AC2 – Action: black with green logo	BC2 – B&C: black with large green logo
AC3 – Action: light grey with blue logo	BC3 – B&C: black with small green logo
AC4 – Action: 'blue singer' logo	CH1 – Charisma: scroll, no B&C credit
BC1 – B&C: black with silver logo	CH2 – Charisma: scroll, B&C credit
BC2 – B&C: black with green logo	CH3 – Charisma: large Mad Hatter
CH1 – Charisma: scroll, no B&C credit	CH4 – Charisma: small Hatter, full B&C credit
CH2 – Charisma: scroll, B&C credit	CH5 – Charisma: small Hatter, "Marketed" credit
CH3 – Charisma: Mad Hatter, full B&C credit	PE1 – Pegasus: flying horse
CH4 – Charisma: Mad Hatter, "Marketed" credit	PE2 – Peg: clothes peg
PE1 – Pegasus: flying horse	
PE2 – Peg: clothes peg	

Pressing companies used by B&C

The majority of early releases were pressed by Orlake at their Dagenham plant. These have rough–textured labels and matrix numbers in the run–off have "+" between each component, e.g. "CB+100+A". The B&C group of companies also used Philips, whose 7" singles are easily distinguished by three–pronged die–cut centres or large centre holes (Orlake singles have either four–pronged die–cut or solid centres). On Philips pressings, the matrix numbers in the run–off include a double forward slash, such as "CB 122 A//1".

In 1970 B&C switched from Philips/Orlake to EMI. EMI pressings are distinguished by the inclusion of "U" at the end of the run–off matrix number, e.g. "CB 130 A–1U": this appears to indicate EMI pressings for non–EMI companies. The first EMI–pressed single in the CB sequence looks to be CB 129, dating the switch at around August 1970, which seems to be confirmed by September 1970 CAS LP releases being EMI pressings. Although the original pressings of CAS 1018 to CAS 1022 were done by EMI, the 7" singles pressed up to promote the LPs were Orlake pressings – perhaps Orlake was more reasonably priced when it came to small pressing runs.

By late 1974 it looks as though B&C was using any pressing company that would extend it credit. In November 1974, at least some new records and back catalogue repressings on Mooncrest are Lyntone pressings, whilst Saga and CBS were also used (Charisma precluded the uncertainty of supply by shifting manufacture of their own records to Bruin B.V. Zaandam in Holland). It is very difficult to unearth quite what was happening toward the end – B&C tried to keep its cashflow problems secret, but because it did this semi–successfully speculation is rife, whilst hard facts are somewhat thin on the ground. Certainly, over £16,000 was owed to CBS Manufacturing when B&C was wound up.

Sources used in lists

[1] *The New Records* – monthly publication
[2] *New Cassettes & Cartridges* – monthly publication
[3] *The New Singles* – weekly publication
[4] *Music Master* 2nd edition (1976)
[5] *Music Master* 5th edition (1979)
[6] *The Famous Charisma Box – The History of Charisma Records 1968–1985* – booklet from 4–CD boxed set (1993) (yes, EMI got the 25th anniversary wrong)
[7] *Charisma & Pre Complete British Singles: 1970–1984 / B&C Complete British Singles: 1969–1980 / Mooncrest Complete British Singles: 1973–1978 / Pegasus/Peg Complete British Singles: 1971–1972* – compiled, in a ring–bound booklet with listings for other labels, published privately by Paul Pelletier (1995)
[8] Promotional record labels
[9] *Budget Price Records* – quarterly publication
[10] *Cassettes & Cartridges* – monthly publication
[11] *Gramophone Popular Record Catalogue* – quarterly publication
[12] Contemporary music press advertisments

The first three sources above, along with *Budget Price Records*, were published by Francis Antony, whilst the *Music Master* series was published by John Humphries. *Gramophone* and *Cassettes & Cartridges* were published by General Gramophone Publications (the latter, coincidentally, printed by the E.J. Day Group, which also printed many B&C Group record sleeves and ended up being owed over £62,000 when B&C went under). Each source is represented in the listings by superscript numbers: e.g. [1] next to a list item represents that the information was sourced from *The New Records*.

Release and deletion dates

Release dates are sourced, where possible, from contemporary trade publications, *The New Records* and *The New Cassettes and Cartridges*, which were issued monthly, and *The New Singles*, which was issued weekly. The British Library's holdings were used, though many issues are missing. Some gaps were filled from other collections, but it has proven impossible to gain access to thirty or so missing issues. The 1976 *Music Master 2nd Edition* was used to source release dates for LPs only, whilst the *5th Edition* includes listings of all formats, including tape versions. Quarterly publications, *Budget Price Records* and *Gramophone* were used as a last resort, though *Gramophone*'s monthly magazine, *Cassettes and Cartridges*, helped fill a few eleventh hour gaps.

Dates sourced from *The New Records* and *The New Cassettes and Cartridges* often tend to be a month out because both were issued mid–month. For example, an April release notified in March would miss the April edition if that issue had already gone to print. The listing, therefore, would appear in the May edition, itself issued mid–April. Wherever there is a discrepency in release date, all conflicting sources are listed. Where there is no conflict between different sources, only *The New Records* or *The New Cassettes and Cartridges* is shown as source. Where the release date for singles indicates two possible dates a week apart this means that the specific edition and one or more follow–up editions of *The New Singles* were not available during research. *The New Singles* lists releases from the previous fortnight, so depending on whether (and which) subsequent issues are missing you can; a) pinpoint the exact week; b) be left with a two week window; c) have no clue whatsoever if four consecutive editions are missing (which they often are). Where no information was available Paul Pelletier's listings were used. Pelletier's sources comprised *The New Singles, Records of the Month, Pop Singles, Music Week* and the BBC Gramophone Library's record purchasing accounts. Many dates are sourced from promotional copies of the records. There are some interesting mismatches along the way – make of these what you will.

Deletion dates are taken from *Music Master 2nd Edition*, which includes dates for LP deletions advised between 1973 and the end of 1975 and *Music Master 5th Edition*, which includes all deletions advised up to the end of 1978. However, it is worth noting that in *Music Master 2nd Edition* all B&C deletions are listed as March 1974 and all Charisma deletions as March 1975: the whole thing has a look of 'tidying up' about it.

The B&C group started to issue tapes in 1972 and release (and occasional deletion) dates are included for both cassettes and 8–track cartridges. Where the listings state that no tape versions were notified to trade publications it is still just possible that one or two of these albums were issued in these formats. Toward the end of 1974 and early 1975 it looks as though B&C was cherry–picking which LPs to also release on tape – probably based on which were likely to bring in cash sharpish. A combination of needing money quickly and of mounting unpaid bills with suppliers probably didn't help matters.

There are one or two potentially confusing issues when it comes to tape releases. Firstly, B&C label CAS series LPs had their tape versions released on the Peg label, to which B&C artists had been transferred the previous year (well, they'd been transferred to Pegasus to be exact, but this had already metamorphosed into Peg). Secondly, when Pegasus/Peg label LPs were reissued on Mooncrest, tape versions were not reissued simply because there were very large stocks of original Pegasus/Peg tapes still available.

Existing stocks of B&C–era tapes became available via the resurrected Mooncrest/B&C/Trojan as from 1976. 8–tracks still remaining on catalogue were deleted when this format ceased to be commercially available in the UK (probably 1979). In fact, many still–sealed 8–track versions crop up on eBay. If no–one else ultimately did well out of B&C, it looks like Precision Tapes did – they certainly didn't end up as one of B&C's many creditors!

Recommended retail price

Prices for LPs and tapes are sourced from *The New Records, The New Cassettes and Cartridges* and the *Music Master* publications. Generally, the prices shown in *The New Records* and *The New Cassettes and Cartridges* are correct and so these are used as the main source. *Music Master* prices are shown where no other price source was available or where the price differs from that shown in *The New Records* and so on.

Where there is only the difference of 1p in stated RRP in different sources – e.g. £2.14 as against £2.15 for LPs – I haven't bothered to document this. Just bear in mind that wherever *The New Records* states £2.15, *Music Master*, if it includes a price, says £2.14 fairly consistently. Adding this discrepency in each individual case made for some very messy listings but didn't really add much value, hence the decision not to document except here. However, a 4p discrepency is a different matter – I mean, that's almost a Shilling!

Discographies

Labels are listed in the order in which they first released records. Therefore, the listings begin with the Action label (first release 1968) and finish with the Seven Sun label (first B&C–related release scheduled for June 1975). LP catalogue sequences are listed first, followed by 7" catalogue sequences and promotional records, irrespective of whether the first issue on any particular label was an LP or single: this is done purely to provide the book with a less chaotic structure. The labels covered are, in order of appearance: Action; Stable; B&C/Charisma; Pegasus/Peg; Mooncrest; People; Dragon; Sussex; Seven Sun. Trojan and related labels are not covered but Dragon is included because, although a reggae label, it was a sub–label of Mooncrest, rather than of Trojan. These listings are not concerned with records released after B&C's liquidation so do not include subsequent Mooncrest or B&C label releases issued by the relaunched B&C Recordings Ltd.

Just to confuse the issue B&C shared its main CAS and CB sequences with Charisma. Therefore the B&C and Charisma labels are listed in the same section with LP sequences shown in order of first release irrespective of whether it was a joint catalogue sequence, B&C–only sequence or Charisma–only sequence – after all, things got very complicated when the Charisma Perspective series started to issue B&C and Pegasus/Peg label material on the Charisma label. Post–B&C Charisma listings can be found in *The Famous Charisma Discography*, an earlier publication in the *Famous British Record Labels* series.

Action

Releases for the Action label were chosen by John Abbey, a noted blues and soul expert, and as far as cherry–picking goes, the original incarnation of the label takes some beating. Almost every record is a classic, and collectors are well aware that the records do not come cheaply. The label petered out in late 1970, which would seem to coincide with Abbey starting the Contempo label, along with the like–minded Bob Kilborn. Contempo followed the same model as Action – Abbey and Kilborn licensed music from the US Roker, Canyon, Soul Clock and RRG labels, but for release via Polydor's new Mojo imprint rather than via B&C or Action. The Action label was revived in 1971 but whether Abbey was still involved is unlikely and, again, the label petered out in mid–1972. It was revived yet again in mid–1973, but in 1974 became dormant again – perhaps because Action–style artists were now being licensed to the newer (and rather more 'hip') People label. Its final revival was in 1975, this time as an 'ethnic' reggae outlet.

Issues from 1968 to 1970 included information on the label as to which US label had licensed the tracks to B&C: when the label was revived in 1971, very few records followed this example.

ACLP/ACLS sequence LPs

All LPs in this sequence were on the orange/yellow label design. All bar the Z.Z. Hill, Al Greene and Jimmy Reed LPs were mono releases only. Only the Z.Z. Hill album is listed with both stereo and mono versions[1], though the 1970 B&C/Action/Stable catalogue lists stereo releases only for all three. All Action LPs were listed as available in the 1970 catalogue but all had been deleted by 1974[4].

The B&C Discography: 1968 to 1975

ACLP 6001
1. Boogaloo Down Broadway
2. Cool Broadway
3. Barefootin'
4. The Bounce
5. Land Of 1,000 Dances
6. Shout Bamalama

THE FANTASTIC JOHNNY 'C': Boogaloo Down Broadway
1. Got What You Need
2. Baby I Need You
3. (She's) Some Kind Of Wonderful
4. Stand By Me
5. New Love
6. Warm And Tender Love

Rel: 1968 or 1969
RRP: not advised

ACLP 6002
1. Oh How It Hurts
2. Poor Girl In Trouble
3. I Need Love
4. You Can Depend On Me
5. I Do Love You
6. Game Of Love

BARBARA MASON: Oh How It Hurts
1. Yes, I'm Ready
2. If You Don't
3. Is It Me
4. Forever
5. I Don't Want To Lose You
6. For Your Love

Rel: 1968 or 1969
RRP: not advised

ACLP 6003
1. Dry Your Eyes
2. Walk On By
3. God Only Knows
4. Who's Loving You
5. Summertime
6. Where Did Our Love Go

BRENDA AND THE TABULATIONS: Dry Your Eyes
1. Just Once In A Lifetime
2. Forever
3. Stay Together Young Lovers
4. Hey Boy
5. Oh Lord What Are You Doing To Me
6. The Wash

Rel: 1969
RRP: not advised

ACLP/ACLS 6004
1. When Something Is Wrong With My Baby
2. What Am I Living For
3. Nothing Takes The Place Of You
4. Knock On Wood
5. Steal Away
6. You Gonna Make Me Cry

Z.Z. HILL: Whole Lot Of Soul (MONO/STEREO)
1. You Send Me
2. Midnight Hour
3. When A Man Loves A Woman
4. Make Me Yours
5. Nothing Can Change The Love I Have For You
6. Greatest Love

Rel: Mar 1969[1]
RRP: 37/5[1]

Although both mono and stereo versions are listed in The New Records, there doesn't otherwise seem to be corroboration of a mono version existing.

ACLP 6005
1. Competition Ain't Nothing (Carl Carlton)
2. Please (Joe Hinton)
3. Sockin' 1–2–3–4 (John Roberts)
4. It's All Over Now (Clarence Carter And Calvin Thomas)
5. Mr Soul (Bud Harper)
6. Tell Him No (The Bell Brothers)
7. No Cure For The Blues (The Lamp Sisters)
8. Spicks and Specks (Bobby Day)

VARIOUS ARTISTS: Action Packed Soul Volume 1
1. Dancin' Man (Ernie K Doe)
2. Share Your Love With Me (Bobby Bland)
3. Something's Got A Hold On Me (Jeanette Williams)
4. That's All A Part Of Loving You (Al 'TNT' Braggs)
5. Baby I Need Your Love (Bobby Williams)
6. Heartaches, Heartaches (O.V. Wright)
7. You're Almost Tuff (Roy Head)
8. Grab Your Clothes (Minnie Epperson)

Rel: Apr 1969[1]
RRP: 37/5[1]

ACLP 6006
1. Back In The Same Old Bag
2. Share Your Love With Me
3. Poverty
4. If You Could Read My Mind
5. Dust Got In Daddy's Eyes
6. These Hands

BOBBY BLAND: A Piece Of Gold
1. Piece Of Gold
2. Save Your Love For Me
3. Who Will The Next Fool Be
4. Good Time Charlie
5. How Does A Cheating Woman Feel
6. Yield Not To Temptation

Rel: Mar 1969[1]
RRP: 37/5[1]

The B&C Discography: 1968 to 1975

ACLP 6007   BETTY HARRIS: Soul Perfection

1. Ride Your Pony
2. What A Sad Feeling
3. Bad Luck
4. I'm Gonna Git Ya
5. Show It
6. Can't Last Much Longer
7. I Don't Wanna Hear It
8. Sometime

1. Mean Man
2. Lonely Hearts
3. Hook Line N Sinker
4. What'd I Do Wrong
5. Trouble With My Lover
6. Nearer To You
7. I'm Evil Tonight
8. 12 Red Roses

Rel: May 1969[1]
RRP: 37/5[1]

ACLS 6008   AL GREENE: Back Up Train (STEREO)

1. Back Up Train
2. Hot Wire
3. Stop And Check Myself
4. Let Me Help You
5. I'm Reachin' Out
6. Don't Hurt Me No More

1. Lovers Hideaway
2. Don't Leave Me
3. What's It All About
4. I'll Be Good To You
5. Guilty
6. That's All It Takes (Lady)
7. Get Yourself Together

Rel: Jun/Jul '69[1]
RRP: 37/5[1]

ACLP 6009   VARIOUS ARTISTS: These Kind Of Blues Volume One

1. Tennessee Woman (Fention Robinson)
2. Little Boy Blue (Bobby Bland)
3. Okie Dokie Stomp (Clarence "Gatemouth" Brown)
4. Texas Flood (Larry Davis)
5. Hound Dog (Willie Mae Thornton)
6. Pledging My love (Johnny Ace)
7. You Got Money (Clarence "Gatemouth" Brown)
8. These Kind Of Blues Pt 1 (Junior Parker)

1. These Kind Of Blues Pt 2 (Junior Parker)
2. She's Gone (Jimmy McCracklin)
3. You've Got To Pass This Way Again (Fention Robinson)
4. Bobby's Blues (Bobby Bland)
5. Just Before Dawn (Clarence "Gatemouth" Brown)
6. That's Alright (Junior Parker)
7. Keep On Doggin' (Roscoe Gordon)
8. Stormy Monday Blues (Bobby Bland)

Rel: Oct 1969[1]
RRP: 37/5[1]

ACLP 6010   GENE CHANDLER: Live On Stage

1. Rainbow '65
2. If You Can't Be True
3. Soul Hootenanny
4. Monkey Time
5. What Now

1. Just Be True
2. Ain't No Use
3. Bless Our Love
4. A Song Called Soul

Rel: Jul 1969[1]
RRP: 37/5[1]

Side 1 label includes the credit "Introduction – Pervis Spann" and side 2 label includes the credit "Introduction – E. Rodney Jones". This was originally issued on the US Constellation label in 1965 as *Live On Stage In '65*.

ACLS 6011   JIMMY REED: Down In Virginia (STEREO)

1. Sugar Sugar Woman
2. Don't Light My Fire
3. Slow Walking Mama
4. Jump And Shout
5. Down In Virginia

1. Check Yourself
2. I Shot An Arrow To The Sky
3. Ghetto Woman Blues
4. Big Boss Lady
5. I Need You So
6. The Judge Should Know

Rel: Oct 1969[1]
RRP: 37/5[1]

Insert. The front sleeve includes a stereo credit on all copies viewed during research. However, stereo copies are known to have "ACLP" (mono) matrix numbers in the run-off. This may just be because B&C didn't usually bother to give different catalogue prefixes to stereo records. In fact this Action LP sequence seems to be the only sequence where a distinction was made – on labels and sleeves at any rate, if not in matrix numbers.

ACMP sequence LP

Despite the Action label logo on the sleeve, the labels were of the current B&C black/green design. Action ceased releasing records in early 1970 and was restarted in late 1971. The following LP was the only LP release from Action's second wave of releases and was the last LP issued on the label, which concentrated thereafter on singles.

ACMP 100   **EDDIE 'GUITAR' BURNS: Bottle Up And Go**
1. She's In L.A
2. Bottle Up And Go
3. Cross Your Heart
4. Detroit Women (Lookey Here Babe)
5. Bad Bad Whisky

1. Kansas City
2. Whisky Headed Woman
3. Your Daddy Ain't Foolin'
4. Vicksburg Blues
5. I Call It Love

Label: BC3
Rel: Oct 1972[1]
RRP: £1.42[4]
£2.25[1]

ACT 4500 sequence 7" singles

The 1970 B&C/Action/Stable catalogue lists all releases up to ACT 4553 as being still on catalogue, except for ACT 4521, which was listed as not issued. One or two records released on the first label design are confirmed as also existing on the second label design. Given that all first label design records were available in 1970, more than those confirmed may exist on the second label design.

ACT 4500   **WILMER AND THE DUKES: Give Me One More Chance / Get It**
Label: AC1   Rel: 20 Sep 1968[3]

ACT 4501   **LITTLE CARL CARLTON: Competition Ain't Nothing / Three Way Love**
Label: AC1   Rel: 20 Sep 1968[3]

ACT 4502   **ERNIE K. DOE: Dancing Man / Later For Tomorrow**
Label: AC1   Rel: 20 Sep 1968[3]

ACT 4503   **MINNIE EPPERSON: Grab Your Clothes (And Get On Out) / No Love At All**
Label: AC1   Rel: 20 Sep 1968[3]

ACT 4504   **BUDDY ACE: Got To Get Myself Together / Darling Depend On Me**
Label: AC1   Rel: 4 Oct 1968[3]

ACT 4505   **O.V. WRIGHT: Oh Baby Mine / Working Your Game**
Label: AC1   Rel: 4 Oct 1968[3]

ACT 4506   **AL "TNT" BRAGGS: Earthquake / How Long (Do You Hold On)**
Label: AC1   Rel: 4 Oct 1968[3]
Four-prong die-cut centre copies have the usual orange colour labels, whilst solid centred copies have a distinct red colour to the labels.

ACT 4507   **HARMONICA FATS: Tore Up / I Get So Tired**
Label: AC1   Rel: 15 Nov 1968[3]

ACT 4508   **VERNON GARRETT: Shine It On / Things Are Looking Better**
Label: AC1   Rel: 25 Oct 1968[3]

The B&C Discography: 1968 to 1975

ACT 4509 BOBBY WILLIAMS: Baby I Need Your Love / Try It Again
Label: AC1 Rel: 15 Nov 1968[3]

ACT 4510 THE BELL BROTHERS: Tell Him No / Throw Away The Key
Label: AC1 Rel: 15 Nov 1968[3]

ACT 4511 JOHN ROBERTS: I'll Forget You / Be My Baby
Label: AC1 Rel: unknown

ACT 4512 ERNIE K-DOE: Gotta Pack My Bags / How Sweet You Are
Label: AC1 Rel: unknown

ACT 4513 THE BROTHERS TWO: Here I Am In Love Again / I'm Tired Of You Baby
Label: AC1 Rel: 6 Dec 1968[3]

ACT 4514 LITTLE CARL CARLTON: 46 Drums, 1 Guitar / Why Don't They Leave Us Alone
Label: AC1 Rel: 6 Dec 1968[3]

ACT 4515 ROOSEVELT GRIER: People Make The World / Hard To Forget
Label: AC1 Rel: 6 Dec 1968[3]

ACT 4516 RUBAIYATS: Omar Khayyam / Tomorrow
Label: AC1 Rel: unknown

ACT 4517 CHUCK TROIS AND THE AMAZING MAZE: Call On You / The Woodsman
Label: AC1 Rel: unknown

ACT 4518 ROY LEE JOHNSON: So Anna You Love Me / ROY LEE JOHNSON AND HIS BAND: Boogaloo No. 3 (Instrumental)
Label: AC1 Rel: 24 Jan 1969[3]

ACT 4519 EDDIE BUSTER FOREHAND: Young Boy Blues / You Were Meant For Me
Label: AC1 Rel: 17 Jan 1969[3]
B-side title not confirmed – of the two variations listed in various places this sounds most likely.

ACT 4520 ALICE CLARK: You Got A Deal / Say You'll Never Leave Me
Label: AC1 Rel: 7 Mar 1969[3]

ACT 4521 NO RELEASE
The B&C/Action/Stable catalogue for 1970 confirms no release on this catalogue number.

ACT 4522 DEE DEE SHARP: What Kind Of Lady / You're Gonna Miss Me (When I'm Gone)
Label: AC1 Rel: 14 Feb 1969[3]

ACT 4523 THE INTRUDERS: Slow Drag / So Glad I'm Yours
Label: AC1 Rel: 10 Jan 1969[3]

The B&C Discography: 1968 to 1975

ACT 4524   BOBBY BLAND: Rockin' In The Same Old Boat / Wouldn't You Rather Have Me?
Label: AC1   Rel: 10 Jan 1969[3]

ACT 4525   DELLA HUMPHREY: Don't Make The Good Girls Go Bad / Your Love Is All I Need
Label: AC1   Rel: 24 Jan 1969[3]

ACT 4526   AL "TNT" BRAGGS: I'm A Good Man/I Like What You Do To Me
Label: AC1   Rel: 7 Mar 1969[3]

ACT 4527   O.V. WRIGHT: I Want Everyone To Know / I'm Gonna Forget About You
Label: AC1   Rel: 7 Mar 1969[3]

ACT 4528   LITTLE RICHARD AND HIS BAND: Baby What You Want Me To Do (Pt. 1) / Baby What You Want Me To Do (Pt. 2)
Label: AC1   Rel: 14 Feb 1969[3]

ACT 4529   NORMAN JOHNSON AND THE SHOWMEN: You're Everything / Our Love Will Grow
Label: AC1   Rel: unknown

ACT 4530   THE PRIME MATES: Hot Tamales (Part 1) / Hot Tamales (Part 2)
Label: AC1   Rel: unknown

ACT 4531   MELVIN DAVIS: Save It (Never Too Late) / This Love Was Meant To Be
Label: AC1   Rel: 2 May 1969[3]

ACT 4532   Z.Z. HILL: Make Me Yours / What Am I Living For?
Label: AC1   Rel: unknown

ACT 4533   BOBBY MARCHAN: Ain't No Reason For Girls To Be Lonely / Ain't No Reason For Girls To Be Lonely (Instrumental)
Label: AC1   Rel: 2 May 1969[3]

ACT 4534   JEANETTE WILLIAMS: Stuff / You Gotta Come Through
Label: AC1   Rel: 23 May 1969[3]

ACT 4535   BETTY HARRIS: Ride Your Pony / Trouble With My Lover
Label: AC1   Rel: 17 May 1969[3]

ACT 4536   EDDIE WILSON: Shing–A–Ling Stroll [see below] / Don't Kick The Teenager Around
Label: AC1   Rel: 13 June or 20 June 1969[3]
Early labels are incorrectly credited as "Shing–A–King Stroll".

ACT 4537   CARL CARLTON: Look At Mary Wonder / Bad For Each Other
Label: AC1   Rel: 13 June or 20 June 1969[3]

ACT 4538   BOBBY BLAND: Gotta Get To Know You / Baby I'm On My Way
Label: AC1   Rel: 13 June or 20 June 1969[3]

The B&C Discography: 1968 to 1975

ACT 4539 THE OLYMPICS: Baby Do The Philly Dog / Mine Exclusively
Label: AC1 Rel: 27 Jun 1969[3]

ACT 4540 AL GREENE: Don't Hurt Me No More / Get Yourself Together
Label: AC1 Rel: 18 Jul 1969[3]

ACT 4541 BRENDA AND THE TABULATIONS: That's In The Past / I Can't Get Over You
Label: AC1 Rel: 18 Jul 1969[3]

ACT 4542 BARBARA MASON: Slipping Away / Half A Love
Label: AC1 Rel: unknown

ACT 4543 THE FANTASTIC JOHHNY C: Is There Anything Better Than Making Love / New Love
Label: AC1 Rel: unknown

ACT 4544 JACKIE LEE AND DELORES HALL: Whether It's Right Or Wrong / Baby I'm Satisfied (NOT RELEASED)
ACT 4544 THE HIDEAWAYS: Hideout / Jolly Joe
Label: see below Rel: 24 Oct 1969[3]
Catalogue number originally assigned to *Whether It's Right Or Wrong / Baby I'm Satisfied* by Jackie Lee and Delores Hall, which was instead issued on B&C as CB 105 with "ACT 4544" crossed out in the run–off. Confirmed on second label design, but if release date is correct, then this must exist on the first label design.

ACT 4545 NORMAN JOHNSON AND THE SHOWMEN: Take It Baby / In Paradise
Label: AC1 Rel: 19 Sep 1969[3]
The US Swan label issue was credited to "The Showmen" alone.

ACT 4546 THE WASH HOPSON SINGERS: He's Got A Blessing / Rocking In A Weary Land
Label: AC1 Rel: 18 Jul 1969[3]

ACT 4547 EDDIE HOLMAN: I Love You / I Surrender
Label: AC1 Rel: 22 Aug 1969[3]

ACT 4548 BOBBY BLAND: Share Your Love With Me / Honey Child
Label: pres. AC1 Rel: 22 Aug 1969[3]

ACT 4549 CLIFFORD CURRY: She Shot A Hole In My Soul / We're Gonna Hate Ourselves In The Morning
Label: AC1 Rel: 3 Oct 1969[3]

ACT 4550 CLIFTON CHENIER: Black Girl / Frog Legs
Label: Rel: 31 Oct 1969[3]

ACT 4551 GENE CHANDLER: I Can't Save It / I Can Take Care Of Myself
Label: pres. AC1 Rel: 24 Oct 1969[3]

ACT 4552 THE PERFORMERS: I Can't Stop You / L.A. Stomp
Label: AC1 Rel: 31 Oct 1969[3]

The last single on the orange label design? Also exists on the black/green design. Orange label copies credit "Mirwood Recording" whilst black/green label copies credit "Crestview/Mirwood Recording".

ACT 4553   **BOBBY BLAND: Chains Of Love / Ask Me 'Bout Nothing But The Blues**
Label: AC2   Rel: 21 Nov 1969[3]

ACT 4554   **NO RELEASE**

ACT 4555   **EDDIE WILSON: Get Out On The Street / Must Be Love**
Label: AC2   Rel: 13 Feb 1970[3]

ACT 4556   **THE OLYMPICS: I'll Do A Little Bit More / Same Old Thing**
Label: AC2   Rel: 13 Feb 1970[3]

ACT 4557   **JEANETTE WILLIAMS: Hound Dog / I Can Feel A Heartbreak**
Label: AC2   Rel: 27 Feb 1970[3]

ACT 4600 sequence 7" singles

The end of the 4500 sequence almost certainly represents the point at which John Abbey ceased his involvement with B&C/Action and moved on to Polydor via the Contempo label. After a year and a half the label was revived along the same lines but now with a few reggae releases dotted amongst the usual soul fare.

ACT 4601   **NORMAN JOHNSON AND THE SHOWMEN: You're Everything / Our Love Will Grow**
Label: AC2   Rel: 1 Oct 1971[3]
Reissue of ACT 4529

ACT 4602   **BILLY SHA-RAE: Do It / Crying Clown**
Label: AC2   Rel: 5 Nov 1971[3]
Copies exist with both four prong die-cut and solid centres.

ACT 4603   **BOBBETTES: That's A Bad Thing To Know / All In Your Mind**
Label: AC2   Rel: 14 Jan[8]/28 Jan 1972[3]

ACT 4604   **BOBBY PATTERSON: I'm In Love With You / Married Lady**
Label: AC2   Rel: 3 Mar[3]/7 Apr 1972[3]

ACT 4605   **HOAGY LANDS: Why Didn't You Let Me Know / Do You Know What Life Is All About**
Label: AC2   Rel: 19 May 1972[3]

ACT 4606   **KIM FOWLEY: Born To Make You Cry / Thunder Road**
Label: AC2   Rel: 3 May[3]/21 Jul[8]/4 Aug 1972[3]
Stock copies exist with solid centres.

ACT 4607   **JOE S. MAXEY: Sign Of The Crab / May The Best Man Win**
Label: AC2   Rel: May 1973[5]

ACT 4608   **THE SINGING PRINCIPAL: Thank You Baby / Women's Lib**
Label: AC2   Rel: 4 May 1973[8]

The B&C Discography: 1968 to 1975

ACT 4609   **EDDIE BO: Check Your Bucket Part One / Check Your Bucket Part Two**
Label: AC3   Rel: 1 Jun 1973[8]
Three variations known: solid-centred promotional copies exist with "DEMO RECORD NOT FOR SALE" text and tracks the same as on the normal stock release; four prong die-cut centred promotional copies exist with just a large block "A" and tracks the same as on the normal stock release; normal die-cut centred stock copies viewed seem to have much rougher textured labels than the promotional variations.

ACT 4610   **GAYTONES: Soul Makossa Part 1 / Soul Makossa Part 2**
Label: AC3   Rel: 6 Jul 1973[3]
Promotional copies have a large block "A", though otherwise the same as the normal stock release.

ACT 4611   **JAMAICA BAND: Sticky Fingers / Sticky Fingers. Part 2**
Label: AC3   Rel: 17 Aug 1973[3]
Promotional copies exist with a large block "A", though tracks are the same as on the normal stock release, and have a noticeably rougher texture label than other releases around this date. That this is an Orlake pressing, even though B&C was generally using EMI to press records at this point, is confirmed by the "ACT+4611+A" / "ACT+4611+B" matrix numbers in the run-off.

ACT 4612   **BUSTER PEARSON BAND: Big Funk / Pretty Woman**
Label: AC3   Rel: 24 Aug 1973[3]
Promotional copies exist with a large block "A", though with same tracks as on normal stock release.

ACT 4613   **WILBERT HARRISON: Get It While You Can / Amen**
Label: AC4   Rel: 12 Oct 1973[3]

ACT 4614   **5 MILES OUT: Super Sweet Girl Of Mine / Set Your Mind Free**
Label: AC4   Rel: 26 Oct 1973[3]
One-sided white label test pressing exists.

ACT 4615   **STANLEY: I'll Go Down And Getcha Pt 1 / I'll Go Down And Getcha Pt 2**
Label: AC4   Rel: 2 Nov 1973[3]
Promotional copies exist with track listing as above.

ACT 4616   **BACKYARD HEAVIES: Just Keep On Truckin' / Never Can Say Goodbye**
Label: AC4   Rel: 9 Nov[3]/30 Nov 1973[3]
Promotional copies exist with *My Sweet Baby* on both sides though some play normal b-side.

ACT 4617   **MILL EDWARDS: I Found Myself / Don't Forget About Me**
Label: AC4   Rel: 9 Nov 1973[3]

ACT 4618   **THE ESQUIRES: My Sweet Baby / Henry Ralph**
Label: AC4   Rel: 16 Nov 1973[3]

ACT 4619   **AARON McNEIL: Soul Of A Black Man / Reap What You Sow**
Label: AC4   Rel: 16 Nov 1973[3]

ACT 4620   **CHUCK ARMSTRONG: Black Foxy Woman / God Bless The Children**
Label: AC4   Rel: 11 Jan 1974[3]   Del: 1978[5]
Promotional copies exist with *Black Foxy Woman* on both labels, though some play normal b-side.

ACT 4621   **TOM GREEN:** Rock Springs Railroad Station / Endless Confusion
Label: AC4   Rel: 11 Jan 1974[3]   Del: 1976[5]

ACT 4622   **BOBBIE HOUSTON:** I Want To Make It With You / I Want To Make It With You (Instrumental)
Label: AC4   Rel: 11 Jan 1974[3]

ACT 4623   **THE CHOSEN FEW:** Funky Butter / Wondering
Label: AC4   Rel: 11 Jan 1974[3]   Del: 1976[5]

ACT 4624   **WEE WILLIE AND THE WINNERS:** Get Some / A Plan For The Man
Label: AC4   Rel: 19 Apr 1974[3]
Orlake pressings known to exist.

ACT 100 sequence 7" singles

After yet another hiatus, this time of just over a year, the Action label was brought back into service, this time as an output for what B&C and Trojan referred to as 'ethnic reggae'. The label was not resurrected following B&C and Trojan's liquidation.

ACT 101   **BIG YOUTH:** Knotty No Jester / Knotty No Jester (Instrumental)
Label: AC4   Rel: 23 May 1975[3]   Del: 1978[5]
Rumours of copies appearing on Trojan's Attack label by mistake are not confirmed.

ACT 102   **CORNELL CAMPBELL:** Natty Dread In A Greenwich Farm / Natty Version
Label: AC4   Rel: 6 Jun 1975[3]   Del: 1977[5]

ACT 103   **LINVAL THOMPSON:** Natty Dread Girl / Natty Dread Girl (Version)
Label: AC4   Rel: not notified to *The New Singles*

Promotional 7" EP

The BCP sequence was used for promotional singles over various B&C–related labels. Most so far identified were of artists on B&C, Charisma or Pegasus/Peg. Only one record has been discovered with Action label material, and that only on one side with the other dedicated to People label material.

BCP 16   **VARIOUS ARTISTS:** untitled
1. Forever (Don Gardner And Baby Washington)
2. Lonely Days, Lonely Nights (Don Downing)
1. Check Your Bucket (Eddie Bo)
2. Get It While You Can (Wilbert Harrison)
Label: see below

The a-side had the People label design, whilst the b-side was the Action label design (AC3). All tracks are edited versions.

Stable

SLP sequence LP

SLP 7001 THE DEVIANTS: Disposable (MONO)
1. Somewhere To Go
2. Sparrows And Wires
3. Jamie's Song
4. You've Got To Hold On
5. Fire In The City
6. Let's Loot The Supermarket

1. Pappa–Oo–Mao–Mao
2. Slum Lord
3. Blind Joe McTurk's Last Session
4. Normality Jim
5. Guaranteed To Bleed
6. Sidney B. Goode
7. Last Man

Rel: May 1969[1]
RRP: 40/11[1]

Unidentified music paper advert cutting has RRP of 39/11 – RRP as advised above probably incorrect.

SLE sequence LPs

All records listed as stereo in *The New Records* except for SLE 8001. At least two LPs were originally assigned to the B&C label. SLE 8004 was originally assigned to CAS 1004 and SLE 8005 was originally assigned to CAS.1008.

SLE 8001 SAM GOPAL: Escalator (MONO)
1. Cold Embrace
2. The Dark Lord
3. The Sky Is Burning
4. You're Alone Now
5. Grass
6. It's Only Love

1. Escalator
2. Angry Faces
3. Midsummer Night's Dream
4. Season Of The Witch
5. Yesterlove

Rel: Mar 1969[1]
RRP: 37/5[1]

SLE 8002 N.S.U.: Turn Me On, Or Turn Me Down
1. Turn Me On, Or Turn Me Down
2. His Town
3. You Can't Take It From The Heart
4. Love Talk
5. All Aboard

1. The Game
2. Stoned
3. Pettsie's Blues
4. On The Road Again

Rel: Jun/Jul '69[1]
RRP: 37/5[1]

SLE 8003 JAKLIN: Jaklin
1. Rosie
2. Song To Katherine
3. Look For Me Baby
4. Early In The Morning
5. Just Been Left Again

1. The Same For You
2. I Can't Go On
3. Going Home
4. I'm Leaving
5. Catfish Blues

Rel: Oct 1969[1]
RRP: 37/5[1]

SLE 8004 THE VICTIMS OF CHANCE: Victims Of Chance
1. Victims Of Chance, Part 1
2. Victims Of Chance, Part 2
3. Adventures In Tyme
4. Break Away
5. Over And Out (Coda, Side One)

1. Tuesday's Victim
2. L.A. To Frisco – Four Eleven Flat
3. Funky Sunshine
4. Devil's Prayer

Rel: Feb/Mar '70[1]
RRP: 37/5[1]

Licenced from the US Crestview Records label, from which B&C also licensed Bob and Earl.

SLE 8005   **THE GROUP IMAGE: A Mouth In The Clouds**

1. Aunt Ida	1. Hiya	**Rel:** Jul 1970[1]
2. A Way To Love You All The Time	2. Banana Split	**RRP:** 39/11[1]
3. Voices Calling Me	3. My Man	
4. Moonlit Dip	4. Grew Up All Wrong	
5. New Romancing	5. The Treat	

STA sequence 7" single

A single in this sequence by Sam Gopal is rumoured to exist, but no copy has yet come to light so perhaps we can assume that it was not issued. Still, with B&C you never know.

STA 5601   **THE DEVIANTS: You've Got To Hold On / Let's Loot The Supermarket**

Rel: 22 Nov 1968[3]
Demo copies with "SAMPLE COPY NOT FOR RESALE" text credit side 1 as "You Got to Hold On".

Promotional 7" EP

This record was assigned the same catalogue number as the LP that it was pressed to promote. The matrix numbers started a short–lived B&C trend for assigning promotional records with catalogue numbers derived from the artist name, e.g "JH1" and "JH2" for the promotional single for the Jackson Heights Charisma label LP. Promotional singles for the Genesis, Hannibal and Brian Davison LPs received similar treatment.

SLE 8001 SAM GOPAL

1. Escalator	1. Cold Embrace
2. Angry Faces	2. The Sky Is Burning

Includes "DJ COPY NOT FOR RESALE" and "D.J. SAMPLER From SAM GOPAL L.P. 'ESCALATOR'" on labels. Matrix numbers (included on label) are "SG1–A" and "SG1–B". Both sides are published by B&C Music.

B&C and Charisma

B&C and Charisma shared B&C's two main catalogue sequences, CAS and CB, and both labels used the promotional BCP sequence. The vast majority of releases in the CAS and CB sequences were on the Charisma label so (to save on ink) only those records released on the B&C label have this fact indicated with a suffix to the title. All other records on these sequences can confidently be assumed to be Charisma releases.

CAS sequence LPs (B&C and Charisma)

The last B&C record on this sequence was CAS 1045 and, despite 1972 listings in trade publications, B&C supposedly ceased using the CAS sequence in September 1971. The last three CAS numbers assigned to B&C, CAS 1046–1048, were not used, though the albums originally assigned the first two numbers appeared on the Pegasus label with the CAS matrix numbers crossed out in the run–off. This did not represent the first instance of B&C–planned releases being transferred to another label. At least two early releases, CAS 1004 and 1008, were transferred to Stable. All records in this sequence still on catalogue as at decimalisation were listed with RRP of £2.14[4] as at February 1971.

CAS 1001   MERRILL MOORE: Tree Top Tall (B&C)
1. House of Blue Lights – 69
2. Wabash Blues
3. Kansas City
4. Born to Lose
5. Texas In My Soul
6. Bring Me Sunshine

1. Sweet Mama Tree Top Tall
2. Release Me
3. Let the Good Times Roll
4. She Won't Let Me Forget Her
5. Wabash Cannonball
6. Little Green Apples

Label: BC1
Rel: May 1969[1]
RRP: 37/5[1]
Del: Mar 1974[4]

CAS 1002   DION AND THE BELMONTS: Together Again (B&C)
1. Moving Man
2. Berimbau
3. Come To My Side
4. All I Wanna Do
5. But Not for Me
6. New York Town

1. Loserville
2. For Bobbie
3. Jump Back Baby
4. Baby You've Been On My Mind
5. My Girl the Month Of May

Label: BC2
Rel: Oct 1969[1]
RRP: 37/5[1]
Del: Mar 1974[4]

Reissue of HMV label issue, CLP 3618.

CAS 1003   PACIFIC GAS AND ELECTRIC: Get It On (B&C)
1. Wade In The Water
2. Cry, Cry, Cry
3. Motor City's Burning

1. The Hunter
2. Long Handled Shovel
3. Jelly Jelly
4. Stormy Times
5. Live Love

Label: BC2
Rel: Oct 1969[1]
RRP: 37/5[1]
Del: Mar 1974[4]

CAS 1004   VICTIMS OF CHANCE: Victims Of Chance (B&C: NOT RELEASED)
Instead issued on Stable as SLE 8004 with "CAS 1004" crossed out in the run–off.

CAS 1005   RARE BIRD: Rare Bird
1. Iceberg
2. Times
3. You Went Away
4. Melanie

1. Beautiful Scarlet
2. Sympathy
3. Natures Fruit
4. Bird On A Wing
5. God Of War

Label: CH1
Rel: Dec 1969[1]
RRP: 37/6[1]
Del: Mar 1975[4]

The B&C Discography: 1968 to 1975

There is also documentation of a November 1969 release date[6] though this looks to be incorrect. The above-listed December date is most likely, especially as Gail Colson, Charisma's then label manager gives: a release date of December 10th (email dated 2nd July 2009).

CAS 1006   **NO RELEASE (PRESUMABLY INTENDED FOR B&C RELEASE)**

CAS 1007   **VAN DER GRAAF GENERATOR: The Least We Can Do Is Wave to Each Other**

1. Darkness (11/11)
2. Refugees
3. White Hammer

1. Whatever Would Robert Have Said
2. Out Of My Book
3. After the Flood

Label: CH1
Rel: Jan[6]/Feb '70[1]
RRP: 37/5[1]

Two different mixes exist on the original, rough-textured label design. A double-sided poster was included with first mix and some second mix copies. Original mix copies have "CAS+1007+A2" and "CAS+1007+B2" matrix numbers, denoting these to be Orlake pressings. The original mix is fairly odd with vocals, drums, and bass to the fore but little evidence of the organ or saxophone. The ending to *After the Flood* is significantly different, with a complete fade out before the final organ scrunge. Remixed scroll label copies have the matrix numbers "CAS+1007+A+G" and "CAS+1007+B+G". Second mix copies on smooth-textured pink scroll label have "A-3U" and "B-3U" matrix suffixes, denoting these to be EMI pressings. By this time the label includes the B&C credit. B&C-era copies did not include sleeve spine credits. This LP also appears in the Oct 1970 edition of *The New Records* with a price of 39/11. This might indicate the date that the remixed version appeared.

CAS 1008   **THE GROUP IMAGE: A Mouth In The Clouds (B&C: NOT RELEASED)**
Instead issued on Stable as SLE 8005 with "CAS 1008" crossed out in the run-off.

CAS 1008   **JOSEPH EGER: Classical Heads**

1. Lelio (Berlioz/Eger):
   ii Chorus Of The Shades
   iv Fantasia On Shakespeare's Tempest
2. Symphonie Fantastique (Excerpts) (Berlioz/Eger):
   1st Movement
   4th Movement
   5th Century Plain Song

1. Symphonie Fantastique: 5th Movement
2. The Unanswered Question (Ives)
3. Sonata Pia E. Forte (Gabriele)
4. Troika (From Leuitenant Kije)
5. Infernal Dance Of Kastchei (Stravinsky)

Label: CH1
Rel: Mar[6]/Apr '70[1]
RRP: 39/11[1]

Labels credit "The Sinfonia of London with the Ambrosian Singers, words spoken by John Neville". On catalogue long enough to be issued on the large Mad Hatter label (though, oddly, still as an Orlake, rather than EMI, pressing). Listed as still available as at the end of 1975[4].

CAS 1009   **GORDON TURNER: Meditation**

1. A System Of Meditation By Threefold Attunement And Text Spoken By Gordon Turner

1. A System Of Meditation By Threefold Attunement And Text Spoken By Gordon Turner

Label: CH1
Rel: Mar[6]/Apr '70[1]
RRP: 39/11[1]

Subtitled, "A System of Meditation By Three-fold Attunement", this was issued in two different sleeve designs, both of which included a 16 page booklet. The front sleeve of the first issue included a colourful picture of a dragonfly – the front only was laminated; the second (unlaminated) sleeve design was of a window in a bare room. The text and layout on the rear of the sleeve differed between the two designs. The first press in the laminated sleeve was an Orlake pressing, whilst all copies of the second press in the non-laminated sleeve viewed have been Philips pressings. This is one of only two confirmed Philips LP pressings for B&C/Charisma. Neither issue includes B&C label credits. Listed as still available as at the end of 1975[4]. (The follow-up LP, *Sleep*, on the Transatlantic-distributed Elysion label, credits the Charisma LP as "Attunement Meditation".)

The B&C Discography: 1968 to 1975

CAS 1010   ATOMIC ROOSTER: Atomic Rooster (B&C)

1. Friday The 13th
2. And So To Bed
3. Broken Wings
4. Before Tomorrow

1. Banstead
2. S.L.Y.
3. Winter
4. Decline And Fall

Label: BC2
Rel: Mar 1970[1]
RRP: 37/5[1]

Also appears in the October 1970 edition of *The New Records* with a price of 39/11 – and it is possible that this date represents a repromotion of the album following remixing and overdubbing of vocals and guitar. There are generally known to be two versions of the album, one referred to as the "flute mix" and the other as the "guitar mix". The reason for the two mixes is that new member, John Cann, added vocals and guitar to *Friday the 13th* and guitar to *S.L.Y.* and *Before Tomorrow* prior to the album's US release on Elektra. These new versions subsequently replaced the original tracks on the UK issue. However, just to confuse issues, there are actually two different flute mixes to contend with as well, with tracks switched between sides, depending on mix version. There is also a very interesting mispress that mixes both 'flute mix' variations.

There's a lot to unravel about the different versions, but the above track listing represents that as listed on all labels and sleeves – these seem to have remained consistent throughout all variations. This means that sleeve and labels showed an incorrect track listing on the very first press. Exact order of tracks on original copies is not yet confirmed – first 'flute mix' copies (Orlake pressings with "CAS+1010+A"/"CAS+1010+B" matrix numbers in the run-offs) had *Broken Wings* (definitely) and *Before Tomorrow* (probably) on side 2 and *Winter* and *Decline And Fall* (both definitely) on side 1.

The LP seems to have been hurriedly remixed with tracks moved so as to follow the track listing as listed on sleeve and labels (as shown above). This second 'flute mix' is also an Orlake pressing and has "CAS+1010+A2"/ "CAS+1010+B2" matrix numbers in the run–offs – and it is probably worth mentioning that the run–off space is wider on this version than on the original press, the grooves being more compacted. The 'guitar mix' version included the remixed and overdubbed versions of *Friday the 13th, S.L.Y.* and *Before Tomorrow*. All known 'guitar mix' copies are EMI pressings with "CAS 1010 A–1U"/"CAS 1010 B–1U" matrix numbers in the run–off.

One super-rare variation has surfaced recently, which is a hybrid of the two 'flute mix' versions with "CAS+1010+A" matrix on side 1 and "CAS+1010+B2" matrix on side 2. This means that the record has *Winter* and *Decline And Fall* on both sides of the record, with different mixes on each side.

CAS 1011   RARE BIRD: As Your Mind Flies By

1. What You Want to Know
2. Down on the Floor
3. Hammerhead
4. I'm Thinking

1. Flight:
   a. Part 1: As Your Mind Flies By
   b. Part 2: Vacuum
   c. Part 3: New Yorker
   d. Part 4: Central Park

Label: CH2
Rel: Sep[6]/Oct '70[1]
RRP: 39/11[1]

Textured sleeve.

CAS 1012   AUDIENCE: Friend's Friend's Friend

1. Nothing You Do
2. Belladonna Moonshine
3. It Brings a Tear
4. Raid

1. Right On Their Side
2. Ebony Variations
3. Priestess
4. Friend's, Friend's, Friend

Label: CH1
Rel: May[6]/Oct '70[1]
RRP: 39/11[1]

The release date in *The New Records* may represent a renotification of release.

CAS 1013   NO RELEASE (PRESUMABLY INTENDED FOR B&C RELEASE)

CAS 1014   THE NICE: Five Bridges

1. The Five Bridges Suite:
   Fantasia. 1st Bridge
   2nd Bridge
   Chorale. 3rd Bridge
   High Level Fugue. 4th Bridge
   Finale. 5th Bridge

1. Intermezzo, Karelia Suite
2. Pathetique Symphony No. 6
   3rd Movement
3. Country Pie/Brandenburg Concerto No. 6
4. One Of Those People

Label: CH1
Rel: May 1970[1]
RRP: £2.14[4]

The B&C Discography: 1968 to 1975

Cassette: ZCCAS 1014 Rel: Apr 1972[2] RRP: £2.50[2]
8–track: Y8CAS 1014 Rel: Apr 1972[2] RRP: £2.60[2]
One of only two B&C/Charisma LPs to be confirmed with Philips pressings.

CAS 1015   KEITH CHRISTMAS: Fable Of The Wings (B&C)
1. Waiting For The Wind To Rise
2. The Fawn
3. Lorri

1. Kent Lullaby
2. Hamlin
3. Fable Of The Wings
4. Bednotch

Label: BC3
Rel: Nov 1970[1]
RRP: 39/11[1]

Embossed sleeve with photos affixed to front and rear. For those who insist on trivia, the photos were taken in part of Magic Muscle's squat in the Cotham area of Bristol.

CAS 1016   HAROLD McNAIR: The Fence (B&C)
1. The Fence
2. True Love Adventure
3. Early In The Morning

1. Scarborough Fair
2. Here, There And Everywhere

Label: BC3
Rel: Nov 1970[1]
RRP: 39/11[1]
Del: Mar 1974[4]

Most copies have a torn sleeve where a pink pouch was attached complete with party balloon inside.

CAS 1017   TREVOR BILLMUSS: Family Apology
1. Ground Song
2. Reflections On Lady Macbeth
3. The Viennese Carousel
4. Last September
5. Sunday Afternoon In Belgrave Square
6. Hungarian Peasant Girl
7. Epithaph For Matthew

1. Whoops Amour
2. The Flaming Bossa Nova
3. Casual Friends
4. Pousette
5. Fishing Song
6. Wise Eyes

Label: CH2
Rel: Sep[6]/Oct '70[1]
RRP: 39/11[1]
Del: Mar 1975[4]

Textured sleeve. Neither this (nor the singles, one on Charisma and the other on B&C) sold despite a large recording budget. If this had appeared on Immediate, Harvest or Vertigo, it would now be hailed as a masterpiece. Well, a masterpiece it remains, and with no reissue to date, an obscure and incredibly rare masterpiece, the price of which is starting to reflect its quality and scarcity.

CAS 1018   JACKSON HEIGHTS: King Progress
1. Mr. Screw
2. Since I Last Saw You
3. Sunshine Freak
4. King Progress

1. Doubting Thomas
2. Insomnia
3. Cry Of Eugene

Label: CH2
Rel: Oct[6]/Nov '70[1]
RRP: 39/11[1]
Del: Mar 1975[4]

CAS 1019   SHELAGH McDONALD: Album (B&C)
1. Mirage
2. Look Over The Hill And Far Away
3. Crusoe
4. Waiting For The Wind to Rise
5. Ophelia's Song (Version 1)

1. Richmond
2. Let No Man Steal Your Thyme
3. Peacock Lady
4. Silk And Leather
5. You Know You Can't Lose

Label: BC3
Rel: Nov 1970[1]
RRP: 39/11[1]
Del: Mar 1974[4]

CAS 1020   GENESIS: Trespass
1. Looking For Someone
2. White Mountain
3. Visions Of Angels

1. Stagnation
2. Dusk
3. The Knife

Label: CH2
Rel: Oct[6]/Nov '70[1]
RRP: 39/11[1]

Cassette: ZCCAS 1020 Rel: not advised RRP: unknown
8–track: Y8CAS 1020 Rel: not advised RRP: unknown

The B&C Discography: 1968 to 1975

Original pink scroll and early large Mad Hatter copies issued in textured sleeve with insert on flimsy, lightly-textured, light green paper. The insert was later printed on thicker, white paper.

No tape versions notified to the trade but a B&C-era 8-track cartridge issue is confirmed, which would suggest that a cassette version was also issued – all Charisma product at this point was issued in both tape formats when issued on tape at all. Advertising inner sleeves from July/August 1972 do not list *Trespass* as issued on tape, so quite when the tape versions were released is unknown – perhaps it was in the wake of the success of *Foxtrot*, which was issued in the September.

CAS 1021 BRIAN DAVISON'S EVERY WHICH WAY: Every Which Way
1. Bed Ain't What It Used To Be
2. Castle Sand
3. Go Placidly

1. All In Time
2. What You Like
3. The Light

Label: CH2
Rel: Sep[6]/Oct '70[1]
RRP: 39/11[1]

The record spine credited the LP to "Brian Davison", whilst the back sleeve and the labels credited "Brian Davison's Every Which Way". There was no credit on the front sleeve. Copies exist with the labels affixed to the wrong sides.

CAS 1022 HANNIBAL: Hannibal (B&C)
1. Look Upon Me
2. Winds Of Change
3. Bend For A Friend

1. 1066
2. Wet Legs
3. Winter

Label: BC3
Rel: Nov 1970[1]
RRP: 39/11[1]
Del: Mar 1974[4]

CAS 1023 CAROL GRIMES AND DELIVERY: Fool's Meeting (B&C)
1. Blind To Your Light
2. Miserable Man
3. Home Made Ruin
4. Is It Really The Same

1. We Were Satisfied
2. The Wrong Time
3. Fighting It Out
4. Fool's Meeting

Label: BC3
Rel: Nov 1970[1]
RRP: 39/11[1]
Del: Mar 1974[4]

Appears in the January 1971 edition of *The New Records* with the same RRP (listed under Charisma).

CAS 1024 STEAMHAMMER: Mountains (B&C)
1. I Wouldn't Have Thought (Gophers Song)
2. Levinia
3. Henry Lane
4. Walking Down The Road
5. Mountains

1 Leader Of The Ring
2. Riding On The L And M
3. Hold That Train

Label: BC3
Rel: Nov 1970[1]
RRP: 39/11[1]
Del: Mar 1974[4]

Sleeve included a sticker with album credits and a picture of the band, otherwise there were no credits anywhere on the outer sleeve, though credits appeared on the inner gatefold.

CAS 1025 LINDISFARNE: Nicely Out Of Tune
1. Lady Eleanor
2. Road To Kingdom Come
3. Winter Song
4. Turn A Deaf Ear
5. Clear White Light – Part 2

1. We Can Swing Together
2. Alan In The River With Flowers
3. Down
4. The Things I Should Have Said
5. Jackhammer Blues
6. Scarecrow Song

Label: CH2
Rel: Oct[6]/Nov '70[1]
RRP: 39/11[1]

Cassette: ZCCAS 1025
8-track: Y8CAS 1025
Textured sleeve.

Rel: Apr 1972[2]
Rel: Apr 1972[2]

RRP: £2.50[2]
RRP: £2.60[2]

The B&C Discography: 1968 to 1975

CAS 1026 ATOMIC ROOSTER: Death Walks Behind You (B&C)

1. Death Walks Behind You
2. Vug
3. Tomorrow Night
4. Streets

1. Sleeping For Years
2. I Can't Take No More
3. Nobody Else
4. Gershatzer

Label: see below
Rel: Nov 1970[1]
RRP: 39 /11[1]

One label the usual BC3 design, whilst the other was custom. This author, writing for *The Rough Guide To Rock*, described the LP as, "The album that defined the Rooster image as dark, satanic, leather–clad, moody and magnificent. From the opening freaky piano solo and scrunchy guitar to the final crashing chord, this album is the epitome of heavy rock (as distinct from heavy metal)."

CAS 1027 VAN DER GRAAF GENERATOR: H To He, Who Am The Only One

1. Killer
2. House With No Door
3. The Emperor In His War Room:
   i) The Emperor
   ii) The Room

1. Lost:
   i) The Dance In Sand And Sea
   ii) The Dance In Frost
2. Pioneers Over C

Label: CH2
Rel: Dec 1970[6]/ Jan 1971[1]
RRP: 39/11[1]

CAS 1028 EVERYONE: Everyone (B&C)

1. Trouble At Mill
2. Sad
3. Midnight Shift
4. Don't Get Me Wrong

1. Sitting On A Rock
2. Too Much A Loser
3. Radio Lady
4. This Way Up

Label: BC3
Rel: Feb 1971[1]
RRP: £2.15[1]
Del: Mar 1974[4]

The first CAS LP to be listed with a decimal price. Listed under Charisma in *The New Records*.

CAS 1029 STEELEYE SPAN: Please To See The King (B&C)

1. The Blacksmith
2. Cold, Haily, Windy Night
3. Jigs: Bryan O'Lynn/The Hag With The Money
4. Prince Charlie Stewart
5. Boys Of Bedlam

1. False Knight On The Road
2. The Lark In The Morning
3. Female Drummer
4. The King
5. Lovely In The Water

Label: BC3
Rel: 1971
RRP: prob. £2.15

Cassette: ZCPEG 1029
8–track: Y8PEG 1029

Rel: Jul 1972[2]
Rel: Jul 1972[2]

RRP: £2.25[2]
RRP: £2.35[2]

Hessian–feel sleeve. The insert with explanatory notes was also included (still with B&C credits) with a few early 1974 Mooncrest (CREST 8) copies. By the time the tape versions were issued B&C label artists had been transferred to the Pegasus/Peg label. Therefore this and subsequent tape releases were given the PEG prefix in place of CAS, though retaining their original catalogue number.

CAS 1030 THE NICE: Elegy

1. Hang On To A Dream
2. My Back Pages

1. 3rd Movement Pathetique
2. America 2nd Amendment

Label: CH2
Rel: Apr[6]/May '71[1]
RRP: £2.15[1]

Cassette: ZCCAS 1030
8–track: Y8CAS 1030

Rel: not advised?
Rel: not advised?

RRP: unknown
RRP: unknown

CAS 1031 GINHOUSE: Ginhouse (B&C)

1. Tyne God
2. I Cannot Understand
3. The Journey
4. Portrait Picture
5. Fair Stood the Wind

1. And I Love Her
2. Life
3. Morning After
4. House
5. Sun In A Bottle

Label: BC3
Rel: Apr 1971[1]
RRP: £2.15[1]
Del: Mar 1974[4]

Listed under Charisma in *The New Records*.

The B&C Discography: 1968 to 1975

CAS 1032 AUDIENCE: The House On The Hill
1. Jackdaw
2. Youre Not Smilin'
3. I Had A Dream
4. Raviole

1. Nancy
2. Eye To Eye
3. I Put A Spell On You
4. The House On The Hill

Label: CH2
Rel: Apr[6]/May '71[1]
RRP: £2.15[1]

Cassette: ZCCAS 1032
8-track: Y8CAS 1032
Inner sleeve. Tape versions do not seem to have been advised to *The New Cassettes and Cartridges*.

Rel: not advised
Rel: not advised

RRP: unknown
RRP: unknown

CAS 1033 MARC ELLINGTON: Rains/Reins Of Changes (B&C)
1. Oh No It Can't Be So
2. On Your Own
3. Saving Grace
4. Song For A Friend
5. Yarrow
6. I'm Leaving (America)

1. Rains/Reins Of Changes
2. The Life You Love
3. Days Used To Be Much Warmer
4. Alligator Man
5. All The Times
6. Blue Suede Shoes

Label: BC3
Rel: Jun 1971[1]
RRP: £2.15[1]
Del: Mar 1974[4]

Top-opening, textured sleeve plus insert.

CAS 1034 ANDY ROBERTS: Home Grown (B&C)
1. Home Grown
2. Just For The Record
3. Applecross
4. John The Revelator
5. Moths and Lizards In Detroit

1. Creepy John
2. Gig Song
3. Queen Of The Moonlight World
4. Lonely In The Crowd
5. The One-Armed Boatman And The Giant Squid

Label: BC3
Rel: Jun 1971[1]
RRP: £2.15[1]
Del: Mar 1974[4]

Gatefold insert.

CAS 1035 TIM HART AND MADDY PRIOR: Summer Solstice (B&C)
1. False Knight On The Road
2. Bring Us In Good Ale
3. Of All The Birds
4. I Live Not Where I Love
5. The Ploughboy And The Cockney
6. Westron Wynde

1. Sorry The Day I Was Married
2. Dancing At Whitsun
3. Fly Up My Cock
4. Cannily Cannily
5. Adam Catched Eve
6. Three Drunken Maidens
7. Serving-Girls Holiday

Label: BC3
Rel: Jun 1971[1]
RRP: £2.15[1]

Cassette: ZCPEG 1035
8-track: Y8PEG 1035

Rel: Jul 1972[2]
Rel: Jul 1972[2] (del: 1977[5])

RRP: £2.25[2]
RRP: £2.35[2]

CAS 1036 BIRTH CONTROL: Birth Control
1. Stop Little Lady
2. Just Before The Sun Will Rise
3. The Work Is Done

1. Flesh And Blood
2. Pandemonium
3. Let Us Do It Now

Label: CH2
Rel: May[6]/Jun '71[1]
RRP: £2.15[1]

CAS 1037 PETER HAMMILL: Fool's Mate
1. Imperial Zeppelin
2. Candle
3. Happy
4. Solitude
5. Vision
6. Re-Awakening

1. Sunshine
2. Child
3. Summer Song (In The Autumn)
4. Viking
5. The Birds
6. I Once Wrote Some Poems

Label: CH2
Rel: Jun[6]/Jul '71[1]
RRP: £2.15[1]

Textured sleeve.

The B&C Discography: 1968 to 1975

CAS 1038 WISHFUL THINKING: Hiroshima (B&C)
1. Hiroshima
2. She Belongs To The Night
3. Mary Goodbye
4. Ever Since I Can Remember
5. We're Going To Change All This

1. Now
2. United States Of Europe 79
3. I Wrote A Song
4. 1984
5. Goodbye Lover

Label: BC3
Rel: 1971
RRP: £2.14[4]
Del: Mar 1974[4]

CAS 1039 ATACAMA: Atacama
1. Fiesta A Himara (Bolivia)
2. El Arbol (Chile)
3. A Las Orillas Del Titicaca (Peru)
4. Atara (Argentina)
5. Ojos Azules (Chile)
6. Canto Del Cuculi (Chile)

1. Yaravi Y Huayno De La Quebrada De Humahuaca (Agentina)
2. Dos Palomitas – Yaravi, Huayno, Cueca (Argentina)
3. El Canelazo (Ecuador)
4. Toccoro (Peru)
5. Por Una Pequena Chispa (Bolivia)
6. Virgenes Del Sol (Peru)

Label: CH2
Rel: Jun[6]/Jul '71[1]
RRP: £2.15[1]
Del: Mar 1975[4]

Originally released in the UK in 1970 on the Music Network Label (MNWL–10P) with a different sleeve.

CAS 1040 LEIGH STEPHENS: Leigh Stephens & A Cast Of Thousands
1. World Famous Soul Transplant
2. Medicine Man
3. Simple Song
4. Handful Of Friends

1. Oh Lord
2. Jumpin' Jack Flash
3. Sweet Love Of Mind
4. Chunk Of Funk

Label: CH2
Rel: Aug[6]/Sep '71[1]
RRP: £2.15[1]

CAS 1041 KEITH CHRISTMAS: Pygmy (B&C)
1. Travelling Down
2. Timeless And Strange
3. Evensong
4. Spanky
5. Poem

1. The Waiting Grounds
2. Song For A Survivor
3. Forest And The Shore

Label: BC3
Rel: Sep 1971[1]
RRP: £2.15[1]
Del: Mar 1974[4]

Exists as two one–sided, white label test pressings (some of these were sent out as review copies to minor reviewers, but showing a certain amount of parsimony some reviewers were sent one side and some the other! Listed as a Charisma release in *The New Records*.

CAS 1042 SPIROGYRA: St. Radigunds (B&C)
1. The Future Won't Be Long
2. Island
3. Magical Mary
4. Captains Log
5. At Home In The World

1. Cogwheels, Crutches And Cyanide
2. Time Will Tell
3. We Were A Happy Crew
4. Love Is A Funny Thing
5. The Duke Of Beaufoot

Label: BC3
Rel: Sep 1971[1]
RRP: £2.15[1]
Del: Mar 1974[4]

Inner sleeve. Exists as two one–sided, white label test pressings, details as for CAS 1041. Listed as a Charisma release in *The New Records*.

CAS 1043 SHELAGH McDONALD: Stargazer (B&C)
1. Rod's Song
2. Liz's Song
3. Lonely King
4. City's Cry
5. Dowie Dens Of Yarrow

1. Baby Go Slow
2. Canadian Man
3. Good Times
4. Odyssey
5. Stargazer

Label: BC3
Rel: Sep 1971[1]
RRP: £2.15[1]
Del: Mar 1974[4]

Inner sleeve. Two one–sided, white label test pressings exist, details as for CAS 1041. Listed as a Charisma release in *The New Records*.

The B&C Discography: 1968 to 1975

CAS 1044   PAUL KENT: Paul Kent (B&C)
1. All Across The Night
2. Do You
3. Don't Seduce Your Best Friend's Wife
4. Cool Surprise
5. Soulful Soldier

1. Upstairs Coming Down
2. Rainy Day
3. Song Of Songs
4. Crying In The Aisles
5. Helpless Harry

Label: BC3
Rel: Sep 1971[1]
RRP: £2.15[1]
Del: Mar 1974[4]

Exists as two one–sided, white label test pressings, details as for CAS 1041. Listed as a Charisma release in *The New Records*.

CAS 1045   HAROLD McNAIR: Harold McNair (B&C)
1. Mento
2. Indecision
3. Lord Of The Reedy River

1. The Hipster
2. Mini Blues
3. Spacecraft
4. The Cottage

Label: BC3
Rel: Feb/Apr '72[1]
RRP: see below
Del: Mar 1976[4]

Cassette: ZCPEG 1045
8–track: Y8PEG 1045

Rel: May 1972[2]
Rel: May 1972[2]

RRP: £2.25[2]
RRP: £2.35[2]

Notified to *The New Records* well after B&C had supposedly moved all bar budget releases to Pegasus. *The New Records* RRP is £2.30, whilst *Music Master*'s is £2.14[4], which is more in line with late 1971 releases. Listed first under Charisma in *The New Records*, then under B&C in April.

CAS 1046   DAVE SWARBRICK AND MARTIN CARTHY: Selections
(B&C: NOT RELEASED)
Issued instead on B&C's Pegasus label as PEG 6.

CAS 1047   SHIRLEY COLLINS AND THE ALBION COUNTRY BAND: No Roses
(B&C: NOT RELEASED)
Issued instead on B&C's Pegasus label as PEG 7.

CAS 1048   NO RELEASE (PRESUMABLY INTENDED FOR B&C RELEASE)
Presumably, the record assigned to this number was assigned to B&C and the release transferred to Pegasus, though this remains unconfirmed.

CAS 1049   MONTY PYTHON: Another Monty Python Record
No track credits on sleeve or labels, other than the crossed out Beethoven credit.

Label: CH2
Rel: Oct[6]/Nov '71[1]
RRP: £2.05[1]

Inner sleeve and three inserts (the *Be a Great Actor Kit*). On original release, the inner sleeve was thin paper, the effects insert thick card, the instructions insert grey, lightly–textured paper, and script insert cream, smooth, thin card. Pink scroll and large Hatter label copies have "Beethoven, Symphony No. 2 In D Minor" crossed out, and "Another Monty Python Record" crudely written with a 1970 publication date. No tape versions listed though it is possible that these were issued later.

CAS 1050   LINDISFARNE: Fog On The Tyne
1. Meet Me On The Corner
2. Alright On The Night
3. Uncle Sam
4. Together Forever
5. January Song

1. Peter Brophy Don't Care
2. City Song
3. Passing Ghosts
4. Train In G Major
5. Fog On The Tyne

Label: CH2
Rel: Sep[6]/Oct '71[1]
RRP: £2.05[1]

Cassette: ZCCAS 1050
8–track: Y8CAS 1050

Rel: Apr 1972
Rel: Apr 1972

RRP: £2.50
RRP: £2.60

Some UK original copies had badly blurred inner gatefold illustrations. Also, some original copies included a large "A" on the a–side, similar to promotional singles of the time – reason unknown.

The B&C Discography: 1968 to 1975

CAS 1051   VAN DER GRAAF GENERATOR: Pawn Hearts
1. Lemming (Including Cog)
2. Man-Erg

1. A Plague Of Lighthouse-Keepers:
   a. Eyewitness
   b. Pictures/Lighthouse
   c. Eyewitness
   d. S.H.M.
   e. Presence Of The Night
   f. Kosmos Tours
   g. (Custard's) Last Stand
   h. The Clot Thickens
   i. Land's End (Sineline)
   j. We Go Now

Label: CH2
Rel: Oct[6]/Nov '71[1]
RRP: £2.05[1]

Cassette: ZCCAS 1051   Rel: Apr 1972[2]   RRP: £2.50[2]
8-track: Y8CAS 1051   Rel: Apr 1972[2]   RRP: £2.60[2]

Early copies with lyric sheet (this is visible briefly on Peter Hammill's electric piano during the Belgian TV studio concert). The original intention was for this to be a double album, similar to Pink Floyd's *Ummagumma*, with solo tracks from Guy Evans, Dave Jackson and Hugh Banton, plus live-in-studio re-runs of old classics. The live studio tracks recorded were *Killer*, *Darkness* and *Squid 1 / Squid 2 / Octopus*, of which only the last is still in existence and is included on the 2005 CD edition of *H To He Who Am The Only One* (7 24347 48882 5). Of the solo pieces, Jackson recorded *Plonker's Theme* and parts of another track, now lost, called *Archimedes Agnostic*, Evans recorded *Angle of Incidents* and Banton recorded *Diminutions*. The three surviving solo tracks are included on the 2005 CD edition of *Pawn Hearts* (7 24347 48902 0).

CAS 1052   GENESIS: Nursery Cryme
1. The Musical Box
2. For Absent Friends
3. The Return Of The Giant Hogweed

1. Seven Stones
2. Harold The Barrel
3. Harlequin
4. The Fountain Of Salmacis

Label: CH2
Rel: Nov[6]/Dec'71[1]
RRP: £2.05[1]

Cassette: ZCCAS 1052   Rel: Apr 1972[2]   RRP: £2.50[2]
8-track: Y8CAS 1052   Rel: Apr 1972[2]   RRP: £2.60[2]

Pink scroll/early large Mad Hatter copies issued in textured sleeve. Autumn 1972 tour labels known to exist, though if these were ever routinely attached to any large Mad Hatter stock LPs is doubtful. Genesis expert, Peter Vickers, has seen one copy with labels attached and one with label unattached.

CAS 1053   BELL AND ARC: Bell And Arc
1. High Priest Of Memphis
2. Let Your Love Run Free
3. Keep A Wise Mind
4. So Long Marianne
5. She Belongs To Me

1. Yat Rock
2. Dawn
3. Children Of The North Prison
4. Everyday

Label: CH2
Rel: Nov[6]/Dec'71[1]
RRP: £2.05[1]

Cassette: ZCCAS 1053   Rel: Apr 1972[2]   RRP: £2.50[2]
8-track: Y8CAS 1053   Rel: Apr 1972[2]   RRP: £2.60[2]

CAS 1054   AUDIENCE: Lunch
1. Stand By The Door
2. Seven Sore Bruises
3. Hula Girl
4. Ain't The Man You Need
5. In Accord

1. Barracuda Dan
2. Thunder And Lightnin'
3. Party Games
4. Trombone Gulch
5. Buy Me An Island

Label: CH2
Rel: Feb 1972[1]
RRP: £2.30[1]

Cassette: ZCCAS 1054   Rel: May 1972[2]   RRP: £2.25[2]
8-track: Y8CAS 1054   Rel: May 1972[2]   RRP: £2.35[2]

Inner sleeve. Two one-sided, white label test pressings exist. Also in the April 1972 edition of *The New Records* with RRP of £2.30.

The B&C Discography: 1968 to 1975

CAS 1055   **SPREADEAGLE: The Piece Of Paper**

1. How Can We Be Lost
2. Brothers In The Sunshine
3. Nightingale Lane
4. Piece Of Paper

1. Nightmare
2. Eagles
3. Scipio
4. Talking To A Sailor

Label: CH2
Rel: Apr[6]/May '72[1]
RRP: £2.08[1]

CAS 1056   **CAPABILITY BROWN: From Scratch**

1. Beautiful Scarlet
2. Do You Believe
3. The Band
4. Garden
5. Liar

1. No Range
2. I Will Be There
3. Redman
4. Day In Day Out
5. Sole Survivor:
   a. Escape
   b. Sole Survivor
   c. Cosmic Ride
   d. Time Machine

Label: CH2
Rel: Apr[6]/May '72[1]
RRP: £2.08[1]

Cassette: ZCCAS 1056
8–track: Y8CAS 1056

Rel: Aug 1972[2]
Rel: Aug 1972[2]

RRP: £2.25[2]
RRP: £2.35[2]

Inner sleeve. White label copies known to exist. The last UK LP issued on the pink scroll label design.

CAS 1057   **LINDISFARNE: Dingly Dell**

1. All Fall Down
2. Planktons Lament
3. Bring Down The Government
4. Poor Old Ireland
5. Don't Ask Me
6. O, No, Not Again

1. Dingle Regatta
2. Wake Up Little Sister
3. Go Back
4. Court In The Act
5. Mandolin King
6. Dingly Dell

Label: CH3
Rel: Sep[6]/Oct'72[1]
RRP: £2.25[1]

Cassette: ZCCAS 1057
8–track: Y8CAS 1057
Inner sleeve and poster.

Rel: Sep 1972[2]
Rel: Sep 1972[2]

RRP: £2.25[2]
RRP: £2.35[2]

CAS 1058   **GENESIS: Foxtrot**

Watchers Of The Skies
Time Table
Get 'Em Out By Friday
Can–Utility And The Coastliners

Horizons
Suppers Ready:
   a. Lovers' Leap
   b. The Guaranteed Eternal
      Sanctuary Man
   c. Ikhnaton And Itsacon And Their
      Band Of Merry Men
   d. How Dare I Be So Beautiful?
   e. Willow Farm
   f. Apocalypse In 9/8 (Co–Starring
      The Delicious Talents Of
      Gabble Rachet)
   g. As Sure As Eggs Is Eggs (Aching
      Men's Feet)

Label: CH3
Rel: Sep[6]/Oct'72[1]
RRP: £2.25[1]

Cassette: ZCCAS 1058
8–track: Y8CAS 1058

Rel: Sep 1972[2]
Rel: Sep 1972[2]

RRP: £2.25[2]
RRP: £2.35[2]

Original issue ("A–1U" and "B–1U" matrix copies) in textured sleeve included either a plain white inner sleeve or the "Charisma puts a little colour in your cheeks" advertising inner (the advertising inner sleeve was most likely *not* included with the very first batch). All early sleeves have "E. J. Day" manufacturing credits and "Marketed by B&C Records Ltd." text. There are some interesting variations over the B&C years:

The B&C Discography: 1968 to 1975

1. Textured sleeve with "Printed & Made by Bruin B.V. – Zaandam/Holland" overprinting the "E. J. Day" credits. Small Mad Hatter labels with "Marketed by B&C Records Ltd." text.
2. Non-textured sleeve with credits as above. Very obviously Dutch-manufactured sleeve and record. Large Mad Hatter labels with "Manufactured and distributed by B&C Records Ltd." text. The various label text elements are laid out differently to UK labels.
3. Obviously Dutch-pressed record as in 2 above but in non-textured UK-looking sleeves with "Bruin B.V." credits.
4. Some copies included in *The Genesis Collection Vol. 2* (CGS 103) in textured sleeves, some in non-textured sleeves. Label design could be any of the three UK designs as well – perhaps the boxed sets represented an exercise in using up all the odds and sods of sleeves and label blanks that happened to hanging around.

CAS 1059   BO HANSSON: *Lord of the Rings*

Leaving Shire	A Journey In The Dark	Label: CH3
The Old Forest/Tom Bombadil	Lothlorien	Rel: Oct[6]/Nov '72[1]
Fog On The Barrow-Downs	Shadowfax	RRP: £2.25[1]
The Black Riders/Flight To The Ford	The Horns Of Rohan/The Battle Of Pelannor Fields	
At The House Of Elrond/The Ring Goes South	Dreams in the Houses Of Healing	
	Homeward Bound	
	The Scouring Of The Shire	
	The Grey Havens	

Cassette: ZCCAS 1059   **Rel:** Jan 1973[2]   **RRP:** £2.50[2]
8-track: Y8CAS 1059   **Rel:** Jan 1973[2]   **RRP:** £2.50[2]
Insert showing Tolkien sitting under a tree.

CAS 1060   ATACAMA: *The Sun Shines Up Above*

1. Aires Del Altiplano (Argentina)	1. Sarkahuai (Bolivia)	Label: CH3
2. Caliche (Chile)	2. La Tarijena (Bolivia)	Rel: Sep[6]/Nov '72[1]
3. La Viditay (Bolivia)	3. Puna (Argentina)	RRP: £2.25[1]
4. A Donde Vai Jilguerito (Chile)	4. Rin Del Angelito (Chile)	Del: Mar 1975[4]
5. El Burrito (Chile)	5. Tarde He Venido (Chile)	
6. Arriba Quemando El Som (Chile)	6. El Volantin (Chile)	

CAS 1061   GRAHAM BELL: *Graham Bell*

1. Before You Can Be A Man	1. Watch The River Flow	Label: CH3
2. The Thrill Is Gone	2. Too Many People	Rel: Jan[6]/Feb '73[1]
3. After Midnight	3. How Long Will It Last	RRP: £2.25[1]
4. Down In The City	4. The Whole Town Wants You Hung	
	5. The Man With Ageless Eyes	
	6. So Black And So Blue	

Cassette: ZCCAS 1061   **Rel:** Sep 1973[2]   **RRP:** £2.35[2]
8-track: Y8CAS 1061   **Rel:** Sep 1973[2]   **RRP:** £2.35[2]
Labels have a 1972 publication date.

CAS 1062   STRING DRIVEN THING: *String Driven Thing*

1. Circus	1. Let Me Down	Label: CH3
2. Fairground	2. Very Last Blue Yodell	Rel: Oct[6]/Nov '72[1]
3. Hooked On The Road	3. My Real Hero	RRP: £2.25[1]
4. Easy To Be Free	4. Regent St. Incident	
5. Jack Diamond	5. There You Are	

Cassette: ZCCAS 1062   **Rel:** Sep 1973[2]   **RRP:** £2.35[2]
8-track: Y8CAS 1062   **Rel:** Sep 1973[2]   **RRP:** £2.35[2]

The B&C Discography: 1968 to 1975

CAS 1063   MONTY PYTHON: Monty Python's Previous Record
1. 'A' Side and Half 'B' Side   1. This Side   Label: CH3
                                                                                      Rel: Dec 1972[6]/
                                                                                      Jan 1973[1]
                                                                                      RRP: £2.25[1]

Cassette: ZCCAS 1063   Rel: Jan 1973[2]   RRP: £2.50[2]
8–track: Y8CAS 1063   Rel: Jan 1973[2]   RRP: £2.60[2]

Inner sleeve. Original issue included a *Teach Yourself Heath* flexidisc in picture sleeve. Side 1 label shows a list of contents from a Harley Street Dentist. Last track on this side is *Eric the Half a Bee*.

Flexidisc tracks included on program 4 of the 8–track version (presumably also included on the cassette version). Tape versions titled exactly the same as the LP version – i.e. "Record".

CAS 1064   JO'BURG HAWK: Jo'burg Hawk
1. Uvoyo (Happiness)   1. African Sun   Label: CH3
2. Elegy For Eden   2. This Elephant Must Die   Rel: Jan[6]/Feb '73[1]
3. The Rolling Of The Bones   3. Beaters   RRP: £2.25[1]
4. Dark Side Of The Moon   4. Hunt
5. War Talk   5. The Elephant Is Dead
6. Africa   6. Nglovu Ephili
                                  7. Yebo Mama
                                  8. Sunset

Cassette: ZCCAS 1064   Rel: Sep 1973[2]   RRP: £2.35[2]
8–track: Y8CAS 1064   Rel: Sep 1973[2]   RRP: £2.35[2]

UK issue of material from South African-only LPs *African Day* (Parlophone PCSJ (D) 12080) and *Africa She Too Can Cry* (Parlophone PCSJ (D) 12087).

CAS 1065   DARIEN SPIRIT: Elegy To Marilyn
1. Tailor   1. Hennessey Gunn   Label: CH3
2. Elegy To Marilyn   2. Long Long Way   Rel: Apr[6]/Mar '73[1]
3. Roads   3. Legacy   RRP: £2.25[1]
4. If You're Old Enough   4. The Man I Am
5. For All The Years   5. Maude
6. It Isn't What You Have

Cassette: ZCCAS 1065   Rel: Sep 1973   RRP: £2.35
8–track: Y8CAS 1065   Rel: Sep 1973   RRP: £2.35

Included stick-on mouth on front sleeve. Some Dutch-pressed copies (6369 931) may have been manufactured for UK distribution – the Dutch issue included UK B&C sleeve credits. Whether Dutch copies included the mouth sticker is unknown – several viewed so far show no evidence of such. Also in the May 1973 edition of The New Records with RRP of £2.14.

CAS 1066   CLIFFORD T. WARD: Home Thoughts
1. Gaye   1. Home Thoughts From Abroad   Label: CH3
2. Wherewithal   2. Where's It Going To End?   Rel: Apr[6]/May '73[1]
3. The Dubious Circus Company   3. Time, the Magician   RRP: £2.14[1]
4. Nightingale   4. Give Me One More Chance
5. Where Would That Leave Me?   5. Cold Wind Blowing
6. The Traveller   6. The Open University
                                  7. Crisis

Cassette: ZCCAS 1066   Rel: Jun 1973[2]   RRP: £2.35[2]
8–track: Y8CAS 1066   Rel: Jun 1973[2]   RRP: £2.35[2]

Copies from June and July 1973 included a sleeve sticker indicating the inclusion of the hit, *Gaye*.

The B&C Discography: 1968 to 1975

CAS 1067   **PETER HAMMILL: Chameleon In The Shadow Of The Night**
1. German Overalls
2. Slender Threads
3. Rock And Role
4. In The End

1. What's It Worth
2. Easy To Slip Away
3. Dropping The Torch
4. (In The) Black Room
5. The Tower

Label: CH3
Rel: Apr[6]/May '73[1]
RRP: £2.14[1]

Cassette: ZCCAS 1067
8–track: Y8CAS 1067
Textured sleeve.

Rel: Sep 1973[2]
Rel: Sep 1973[2]

RRP: £2.35[2]
RRP: £2.35[2]

CAS 1068   **CAPABILITY BROWN: Voice**
1. I Am And So Are You
2. Sad Am I
3. Midnight Cruiser
4. Keep Death Off The Road (Drive On The Pavement)

1. Circumstances (In Love, Past, Present, Future Meet)

Label: CH3
Rel: Jun[1]/Jul '73[6]
RRP: £2.14[1]

Cassette: ZCCAS 1068
8–track: Y8CAS 1068

Rel: Oct 1973[2]
Rel: Oct 1973[2]

RRP: £2.35[2]
RRP: £2.35[2]

Also in the August 1973 edition of *The New Records* with RRP of £2.25.

CAS 1069   **ALAN HULL: Pipedream**
1. Breakfast
2. Justanothersadsong
3. Money Game
4. STD 0632
5. United States Of Mind
6. Country Gentleman's Wife

1. Numbers (Travelling Band)
2. For The Bairns
3. Drug Song
4. Song For A Windmill
5. Blue Murder
6. I Hate To See You Cry

Label: CH3
Rel: Jun[1]/Jul '73[6]
RRP: £2.14[1]

Cassette: ZCCAS 1069
8–track: Y8CAS 1069

Rel: Jul 1973[2]
Rel: Jul 1973[2]

RRP: £2.35[2]
RRP: £2.35[2]

Included a booklet stapled to the centre of the inner gatefold. Also in the August 1973 edition of *The New Records* with RRP £2.25 (and the November 1978 edition at £3.99).

CAS 1070   **STRING DRIVEN THING: The Machine That Cried**
1. Heartfeeder
2. To See You
3. Night Club
4. Sold Down The River

1. Two Timin' Rama
2. Travelling
3. People On The Street
4. The House
5. The Machine That Cried
6. Going Down

Label: CH3
Rel: Aug[6]/Sep '73[1]
RRP: £2.25[1]

Cassette: ZCCAS 1070
8–track: Y8CAS 1070

Rel: Oct 1973[2]
Rel: Oct 1973[2]

RRP: £2.35[2]
RRP: £2.35[2]

CAS 1071   **HOT THUMBS O'RILEY: Hot Thumbs O'Riley**
1. Warm Rumours
2. Currently Cheesing
3. No Flies On Auntie
4. Dust My Shovel
5. Harmless Vibration
6. Cosmic Rot

1. Wicked Ivory
2. Tiptoe Through The Graveyard
3. Sunday in Gopher Gulch
4. Grass For Blades
5. The Decline Of The House Of Lords

Label: CH3
Rel: Jul[6]/Aug '73[1]
RRP: £2.25[1]
Del: Mar 1975[4]

UK issue of the 1972 Finnish LP, *Wicked Ivory* (Love LRLP–52). Although credited to "Hot Thumbs O'Riley", this was really a solo LP by Jim Pembroke from Finnish band Wigwam, who also backed Pembroke on this album. *Grass for Blades* was supposed to have an extra verse, but fades out because the studio ran out of tape. True! No tape versions notified.

The B&C Discography: 1968 to 1975

CAS 1072   LE ORME: Felona And Sorona
1. In Between
2. Felona
3. The Maker

1. Web Of Time
2. Sorona
3. The Plan
4. The Balance
5. Return To Naught

Label: CH3
Rel: Jul[6]/Aug '73[1]
RRP: £2.25[1]

Cassette: ZCCAS 1072
8-track: Y8CAS 1072

Rel: Oct 1973[2]
Rel: Oct 1973[2]

RRP: £2.35[2]
RRP: £2.35[2]

Peter Hammill provided English lyrics for this UK issue.

CAS 1073   BO HANSSON: Magician's Hat
1. The City
2. Divided Reality
3. Elidor
4. Before The Rain
5. Fylke
6. Playing Downhill Into The Downs

1. Findhorn's Song
2. Awakening
3. Wandering Song
4. The Sun (Parallel Or 90°)
5. Excursion With Complications

Label: CH3
Rel: Sep[6]/Oct '73[1]
RRP: £2.25[1]

Cassette: ZCCAS 1073
8-track: Y8CAS 1073

Rel: probably Oct 1973
Rel: probably Oct 1973

RRP: prob. £2.35
RRP: prob. £2.35

UK issue of the Swedish LP, *Urtrollkarlens Hatt* (Silence SRS 4615). Listed in *The NewRecords* as "From Out Of The Magician's Hat". Tape versions not listed, though both confirmed as existing.

CAS 1074   GENESIS: Selling England By The Pound
1. Dancing With The Moonlit Knight
2. I Know What I Like (In Your Wardrobe)
3. Firth Of Fifth
4. More Fool Me

1. The Battle Of Epping Forest
2. After The Ordeal
3. The Cinema Show
4. Aisle Of Plenty

Label: CH3
Rel: Sep[6]/Oct '73[1]
RRP: £2.25[1]

Cassette: ZCCAS 1074
8-track: Y8CAS 1074

Rel: Dec 1973[2]
Rel: Dec 1973[2]

RRP: £2.45[2]
RRP: £2.45[2]

Original release included an inner sleeve, which was very soon replaced with a lyric insert that seemed to change colour, from dark green to tan to near-black, with every pressing. Copies with the original brown inner sleeve are extremely hard to find, to the extent that most collectors do not even know of the inner sleeve's existence. Original copies ("A–1U" and "B–2U" matrix suffixes) have B&C credits on the rear of the sleeve above the printing credits, though this credit was removed on later pressings.

Cassette copies had tracks moved around to make both sides of equal length. Side 2 label claims that *After the Ordeal* appears after *Firth of Fifth*, which it doesn't – it's on side 1. To add to the merriment, many (most?) copies of the cassette cut out in the middle of *Aisle of Plenty*. French Phonogram cassettes (7164 019) with B&C marketing credits including the 37 Soho Square address were available in the UK briefly in 1973 (cassette was listed in a Phonogram UK trade catalogue). Presumably, this was available as a stop-gap because of the fact that there was generally at least a month between LP and tape issues during the B&C era.

CAS 1075   NO RELEASE

CAS 1076   LINDISFARNE: Roll On Ruby
1. Takin' Care Of Business
2. North Country Boy
3. Steppenwolf
4. Nobody Loves You Anymore
5. When the War Is Over

1. Moonshine
2. Lazy
3. Roll On River
4. Tow The Line
5. Goodbye

Label: CH3
Rel: Nov[6]/Dec '73[1]
RRP: £2.25[1]

Cassette: ZCCAS 1076
8-track: Y8CAS 1076

Rel: not notified
Rel: not notified

RRP: prob. £2.45
RRP: prob. £2.45

The B&C Discography: 1968 to 1975

Poster. The photo of Kenny Craddock from inner sleeve and poster was later used on the inner sleeve of Alan White's *Ramshackled* album (Atlantic K 50217). Existence of tape versions confirmed.

CAS 1077   CLIFFORD T. WARD: Mantle Pieces
1. Scullery
2. Not Waving – Drowning!
3. Are You Really Interested?
4. A Sad Cliché
5. To An Air Hostess

1. All Modern Conveniences
2. Wayward
3. Screen Test
4. For Debbie And Her Friends
5. Tea Cosy

Label: CH3
Rel: Nov[6]/Dec '73[1]
RRP: £2.25[1]

Insert. No tape versions notified.

CAS 1078   VARIOUS: The Parlour Song Book
1. Home! Sweet Home! (Valerie Masterson)
2. My Pretty Jane (John Brecknock)
3. Throw Out the Lifeline (The Scholars)
4. A Boy's Best Friend is His Mother (Joseph Law)
5. The Lost Chord (Eric Shilling)
6. Come Home Father (Donna Marie Newman And The Scholars)

1. Oh Mother! Take The Wheel (Valerie Masterson)
2. A Son Of The Desert Am I (Eric Shilling)
3. Won't You Buy Me Pretty Flowers (Donna Marie Newman And The Scholars)
4. Sweet And Low (The Scholars)
5. Loves Old Sweet Song (Valerie Masterson)
6. Excelsior! (Eric Shilling And John Brecknock)

Label: CH3
Rel: Nov[6]/Dec '73[1]
RRP: £2.25[1]

Cassette: ZCCAS 1078   Rel: May 1974[2]   RRP: £2.45[2]
8–track: Y8CAS 1078   Rel: May 1974[2]   RRP: £2.45[2]

A selection of Victorian drawing room ballads and jilt songs presented by Michel R. Turner and Antony Miall, with Miall at the piano and harmonium. *Excelsior!* provides a fine and fitting ending. The eight-year-old Donna Marie Newman had been signed to Mooncrest earlier in 1973, though there is no mention of appearance courtesy of this company, probably because both Charisma and Mooncrest sgared board members at this point.

CAS 1079   DOGGEREL BANK: Silver Faces
1. Introduction (A Line)
2. Industrial Estate
3. Down On The Farm
4. The Chairman
5. Who's That Man?
6. Passacaglia
7. Palaces Of Fun

1. Lullabye
2. Scaffolding Is In
3. Cake–Walk
4. Processional
5. Boardroom Reel
6. Silver Faces – Finale

Label: CH3
Rel: Oct[6]/Nov '73[1]
RRP: £2.14[1]

No tape versions notified.

CAS 1080   MONTY PYTHON: Matching Tie and Handkerchief
1. Free Record Given Away With The Monty Python Matching Tie And Handkerchief

1. Free Record Given Away With The Monty Python Matching Tie And Handkerchief

Label: CH3
Rel: Nov[6]/Dec '73[1]
RRP: £2.25[1]

Cassette: ZCCAS 1080   Rel: not notified   RRP: prob. £2.45
8–track: Y8CAS 1080   Rel: not notified   RRP: prob. £2.45

Die–cut sleeve with hard card 'tie and handkerchief' insert and paper insert. Both inserts had one corner cut off so as not to protrude from the die–cut sleeve. This LP was hugely ambitious, in that it was issued with two sets of grooves on side 2, meaning that one of two different sets of tracks would play depending on where the stylus was placed. Several attempts were made to correctly master this LP – see Michael Palin's *Diaries: 1969 – 1979 The Python Years* for the definitive account of the mastering process and all the problems that led to the side 2 tracks having to be cut in mono.

The B&C Discography: 1968 to 1975

No tape versions notified, though these formats known to exist. The cassette version includes the same label credits as the LP despite being a tape rather than a record. It also includes the side 2 tracks in stereo. 8–track copies are presumably the same.

CAS 1081   **NO RELEASE**

CAS 1082   **NATIONAL YOUTH JAZZ ORCHESTRA:** *National Youth Jazz Orchestra*

1. Gate Crasher
2. Winter Is
3. The Perfumed Garden
4. Hip Flask

1. Doghouse
2. All But One
3. Blues For Tony
4. Walkabout
5. Adam Lay Y–Bounden
6. Holland Walk

Label: CH3
Rel: Oct[6]/Nov '73[1]
RRP: £2.14[1]

No tape versions notified.

CAS 1083   **PETER HAMMILL:** *The Silent Corner And The Empty Stage*

1. Modern
2. Wilhelmina
3. The Lie (Bernini's Saint Teresa)
4. Forsaken Gardens

1. Red Shift
2. Rubicon
3. A Louse Is Not A Home

Label: CH3
Rel: Feb[6]/Mar '74[1]
RRP: £2.25[1]

Cassette: ZCCAS 1083
8–track: Y8CAS 1083
Inner sleeve.

Rel: May 1974[2]
Rel: May 1974[2]

RRP: £2.45[2]
RRP: £2.45[2]

CAS 1084   **ROBERT JOHN GODFREY:** *Fall Of Hyperion*

1. The Raven
2. Mountains
3. Water Song

1. Isault
2. The Daemon Of The World:
   a. The Arrival Of The Phoenix
   b. Across The Abyss
   c. The Daemon
   d. The Wanderer
   e. IHS
   f. Tuba Mirum

Label: CH3
Rel: Mar 1974[1]
RRP: £2.25[1]

Also in the April 1974 edition of *The New Records* with RRP of £2.75. Known to exist as two one–sided, white label test pressings. No tape versions notified.

CAS 1085   **JACK THE LAD:** *It's Jack the Lad*

1. Boilermaker Blues
2. Back On The Road Again
3. Plain Dealing
4. Fast Lane Driver
5. Turning Into Winter

1. Why Can't I Be Satisfied
2. Song Without A Band
3. Rosalee
4. Promised Land
5. A Corny Pastiche (Medley):
   a. The Black Cock Of Whickham
   b. Chief O'Neills Favourite
   c. The Golden Rivet
   d. Staten Island
   e. The Cook In The Kitchen
6. Lying On The Water

Label: see below
Rel: Mar 1974[1]
RRP: £2.25[1]

Cassette: ZCCAS 1085
8–track: Y8CAS 1085

Rel: May 1974[2]
Rel: May 1974[2]

RRP: £2.45[2]
RRP: £2.45[2]

CH4 label design confirmed, but must exist on CH3 if the release date as listed is correct (which it would seem is so).

The B&C Discography: 1968 to 1975

CAS 1086   **SIR JOHN BETJEMAN: Betjeman's Banana Blush**

1. Indoor Games Near
2. Business Girls
3. Agricultural Caress
4. Youth And Age On Beaulieu River Hants
5. The Arrest Of Oscar Wilde At The Cadogan Hotel

1. Newbury Lenten Thoughts
2. The Cockney Amorist
3. Longfellow's Visit To Venice
4. The Flight From Bootle
5. A Shropshire Lad
6. On a Portrait Of A Deaf Man
7. A Child Ill

Label: CH3
Rel: Mar 1974[1]
RRP: £2.25[1]

Cassette: ZCCAS 1086   **Rel:** May 1974[2]   **RRP:** £2.45[2]
8-track: Y8CAS 1086   **Rel:** May 1974[2]   **RRP:** £2.45[2]
Textured sleeve with printed paper inner sleeve.

CAS 1087   **REFUGEE: Refugee**

1. Papillon
2. Someday
3. Grand Canyon:
   a. 1st Movement The Source
   b. 2nd Movement Theme For The Canyon
   c. 3rd Movement The Journey
   d. 4th Movement Rapids
   e. 5th Movement The Mighty Colarado

1. Ritt Mickley
2. Credo:
   a. 1st Movement Prelude
   b. 2nd Movement I Believe
   c. 3rd Movement Theme
   d. 4th Movement The Lost Cause
   e. 5th Movement Agitato
   f. 6th Movement I Believe (Part II)
   g. 7th Movement Variation
   h. 8th Movement Main Theme Finale

Label: CH3
Rel: Apr[6]/May '74[1]
RRP: £2.25[1]

Cassette: ZCCAS 1087   **Rel:** Jun 1974[2]   **RRP:** £2.45[2]
8-track: Y8CAS 1087   **Rel:** Jun 1974[2]   **RRP:** £2.45[2]
Inner sleeve. Track 3, side 1 credited as "Grand Canyon" on sleeve but credited as "Canyon Suite" on inner sleeve and label. The short, uncredited 'intro' to *Ritt Mickley* is credited on the CD reissue as *Gatecrasher*, much to the annoyance of those who think that they are getting an otherwise unreleased bonus track. *Ritt Mickley* named after Patrick Moraz' pronunciation of "rhythmically".

CAS 1088   **BERNARD HAITINK: Ken Russell's Film Mahler**

1. Excerpts From Symphonies:
   a. No. 10 In F Sharp: Adagio
   b. No. 3 In D Minor: Kraftig. Entschieden
   c. No. 5 In C Sharp Minor: Adagietto
   d. No. 4 In G: Bedächtig. Nicht Eilen– Recht Gemächlich
   e. No. 3 In D Minor: Lustif im Tempo Und Keck Im Ausdruck
   f. No. 1 In D: Kräftig Bewegt
   g. No. 6 In A minor: Allegro Energico, Ma Non troppo
   h. No. 7 In E minor: Comodo. Scherzando. Ohne Hast

1. Excerpts From Symphonies:
   a. No. 5 In C Sharp Minor: Trauermarsch (In Gemessenum Schritt. Streng. Wie Ein Konduki
   b. No. 1 In D: Feierlich Und Gemessen, Ohne Zu Schleppen
   c. No. 7 In E Minor: Scherzo
   d. No. 3 In D Minor: Kraftig. Entschieden
   e. No. 5 In C Sharp Minor: Scherzo (Kräftig, Nicht Zu Schnell)
   f. No. 9 In D: Im Tempo Eines Gemachlichen Ländlers. Etwas Tappisch Und Sehr Derb
   g. No. 6 In A Minor: Allegro Energico, Ma Non Troppo

Label: CH3
Rel: Apr 1974[6]

Cassette: ZCCAS 1088   **Rel:** May 1974[2]   **RRP:** £2.45[2]
8-track: Y8CAS 1088   **Rel:** May 1974[2]   **RRP:** £2.45[2]
Label extends the sleeve credit: "Soundtrack Of Ken Russell's Film "The Life Story Of Mahler"". Bernard Haitink conducts the Concertgebouw Orchestra. Released by arrangement with Phonogram.

The B&C Discography: 1968 to 1975

CAS 1089   PETER HAMMILL: In Camera
1. Ferret And Featherbird
2. (No More) The Submariner
3. Tapeworm
4. Again
5. Faint–Heart And The Sermon

1. The Comet, The Course, The Tail
2. Gog
3. Magog (In Bromide Chambers)

Label: CH4
Rel: Aug 1974[1]
RRP: £2.45[1]

Cassette: ZCCAS 1089
8–track: Y8CAS 1089
Inner sleeve.

Rel: Sep 1974[2]
Rel: Sep 1974[2]

RRP: £2.40[2]
RRP: £2.40[2]

CAS 1090   BERT JANSCH: L.A. Turnaround
1. Fresh As A Sweet Sunday Morning
2. Chambertin
3. One For Jo
4. Travelling Man
5. Open Up the Watergate (Let The Sunshine In)
6. Stone Monkey

1. Of Love And Lullaby
2. Needle Of Death
3. Lady Nothing
4. There Comes A Time
5. Cluck Old Hen
6. The Blacksmith

Label: CH5
Rel: Sep 1974[1]
RRP: £2.41[1]

Cassette: ZCCAS 1090
8–track: Y8CAS 1090
Insert.

Rel: Sep 1974[2]
Rel: Sep 1974[2]

RRP: £2.40[2]
RRP: £2.40[2]

CAS 1091   GARY SHEARSTON: Dingo
1. Dingo
2. Back Of Beyond
3. Witnessing
4. I Get A Kick Out Of You
5. The Lighthouse Keeper Of America

1. Seagull And Swan
2. The Ballad Of Blasted Creek
3. Lump In The Bed
4. Aborigine
5. Without A Song

Label: CH5
Rel: Sep '74[6]

Cassette: ZCCAS 1091
8–track: Y8CAS 1091

Rel: Oct 1974[2]
Rel: Oct 1974[2]

RRP: £2.40[2]
RRP: £2.40[2]

CAS 1092   UNICORN: Blue Pine Trees
1. Electric Night
2. Sleep Song
3. Autumn Wine
4. Rat Race
5. Just Wanna Hold You

1. Holland
2. Nightingale Crescent
3. The Farmer
4. In the Gym
5. Blue Pine Trees
6. Ooh! Mother

Label: CH5
Rel: Aug '74[6]

Cassette: ZCCAS 1092
8–track: Y8CAS 1092

Rel: Sep 1974[2]
Rel: Sep 1974[2]

RRP: £2.40[2]
RRP: £2.40[2]

Produced by Dave Gilmour. There is also a mysterious credit of "Waters" as co–writer of several songs. Pete Perrier and Pat Martin from Unicorn, through their association with Gilmour, played on the first demos by a very young and unknown Kathy Bush.

CAS 1093   CLIFFORD T. WARD: Escalator (NOT RELEASED)
Originally assigned to Clifford T. Ward's *Escalator*, though this was eventually issued as CAS 1098. There were obviously quite major changes made in planned content of the album – the single, *Jayne (from Andromeda Spiral)* confidently states (on both sides), "From the forthcoming album, 'Escalator' – CAS 1093". In the event neither track was included on *Escalator* as released on CAS 1098.

The B&C Discography: 1968 to 1975

CAS 1094   **JACK THE LAD:** *The Old Straight Track*

1. Oakey Strike Evictions
2. Jolly Beggar
3. The Third Millennium
4. Fingal The Giant
5. Weary Whaling Grounds
6. King's Favourite/The Marquis
    Of Tullybardine

1. Peggy
2. Buy Broom Buzzems
3. De Havilland's Mistake
4. The Old Straight Track
5. The Wurm

Label: CH5
Rel: Oct[6]/Nov '74[1]
RRP: £2.45[1]

Cassette: ZCCAS 1094   Rel: Nov 1974[2]   RRP: £2.65[2]
8–track: Y8CAS 1094   Rel: Nov 1974[2]   RRP: £2.65[2]

Insert. Included a Charisma competition inner sleeve, where the contestant was asked to unscramble anagrams to reveal six Charisma artists, such as "See Gins" and "Rings in the TV Grind".

CAS 1095   **G. T. MOORE AND THE REGGAE GUITARS:** *G.T. Moore And The Reggae Guitars*

1. Painted Ladies
2. Book Of Rules
3. I'm Still Waiting
4. Bye And Bye
5. Way Over There

1. Move It On Up
2. Thou Shalt Not Kill
3. Bad Johnny
4. Knocking On Heavens Door

Label: CH5
Rel: Oct[6]/Nov '74[1]
RRP: £2.45[1]

Cassette: ZCCAS 1095   Rel: Nov 1974[2]   RRP: £2.65[2]
8–track: Y8CAS 1095   Rel: Nov 1974[2]   RRP: £2.65[2]

CAS 1096   **SIR JOHN BETJEMAN:** *Late Flowering Love*

1. Narcissus
2. The Olympic Girl
3. Invasion Exercise On The
    Poultry Farm
4. The Licorice Fields Of Pontefract
5. A Russel Flint
6. Station Syren

1. Myfanwy And Myfanwy At Oxford
2. In The Public Gardens
3. Eunice
4. Senex
5. Late–Flowering Lust
6. Sun And Fun

Label: CH5
Rel: Nov 1974[6]/
Jan 1975[1]
RRP: £2.45[1]

Included the Charisma competition inner sleeve. The competition deadline was 1st Jan 1975, which would be a bit useless if the January release date is correct. No tape versions notified.

CAS 1097   **STRING DRIVEN THING:** *Please Mind Your Head*

1. Overdrive
2. Without You
3. Josephine
4. Mrs. O'Reilly
5. Man Of Means

1. Black Eyed Queen
2. Keep On Moving
3. Timpani For The Devil
4. To Know You Is To Love You

Label: CH5
Rel: Nov[6]/Dec '74[1]
RRP: £2.45[1]

Cassette: ZCCAS 1097   Rel: Mar 1975[2]   RRP: £2.65[2]
8–track: Y8CAS 1097   Rel: Mar 1975[2]   RRP: £2.65[2]

Run–off has "CAS 1096" crossed out and the correct matrix added.

CAS 1098   **CLIFFORD T. WARD:** *Escalator*

1. The Way Of Love
2. Jig–Saw Girl
3. Escalator
4. Trespass
5. We Could Be Talking

1. A Day To Myself
2. Miner
3. Mr. Bilbo Baggins
4. Cellophane
5. A Sad Affair

Label: CH4
Rel: Feb[1]/Mar '75[6]
RRP: £2.45[1]

Cassette: ZCCAS 1098   Rel: Feb 1975[2]   RRP: £2.65[2]
8–track: Y8CAS 1098   Rel: Feb 1975[2]   RRP: £2.65[2]

With different (and unknown) track listing, this album was originally assigned to CAS 1093.

The B&C Discography: 1968 to 1975

CAS 1099   PETER HAMMILL: Nadir's Big Chance
1. Nadir's Big Chance
2. The Institute Of Mental Health, Burning
3. Open your Eyes (The Locarno Song)
4. Nobody's Business
5. Been Alone So Long
6. Pompeii

1. Shingle Song
2. Airport
3. People You Were Going To
4. Birthday Special
5. Two Or Three Spectres

Label: CH4
Rel: Feb 1975[1]
RRP: £2.45[1]

The back of the inner sleeve advertises Hammill's previous solo LPs and the book, *Killers, Angels and Refugees*, which was published by Charisma Books. No tape versions notified.

CAS 1100   HOWARD WERTH AND THE MOONBEAMS: King Brilliant (NOT RELEASED)

Rel: Feb 1975[1]
RRP: £2.45[1]

The February 1975 edition of *The New Records* listed this LP under this catalogue number. However, the LP remained unreleased for several more months and was later issued as CAS 1104 after Phonogram had taken over manufacturing and distribution duties.

CAS 1101   VARIOUS: Beyond An Empty Dream
1. Jesus Of Long Ago (Clifford T. Ward)
2. Give Us the Peace (Anawim)
3. Take This Heart (The Charterhouse Choral Society)
4. Guru (John McLaughlin)

1. Lady Of Sorrow (Anawim)
2. Mother Teresa's Prayer (Anawim)
3. The Man Who Turned On The World (The Friends Of St. Francis)
4. The Waking Song (Anawim)
5. The Name Of Truth (John McLaughlin)
6. Show Me The Man (Anawim)
7. Sympathy (Capability Brown)

Label: CH4
Rel: Apr[6]/Mar '75[1]
RRP: £2.45[1]

Cassette: ZCCAS 1101   **Rel:** May 1975[2]   **RRP:** £2.65[2]
8-track: 8YCAS 1101   **Rel:** May 1975[2]   **RRP:** £2.65[2]

Some with Phonogram sticker over B&C sleeve credit, though with the label still credited to B&C. Subtited "Songs For A Modern Church", which has caused some confusion because this part of the title was used again in 1983 as the title of a follow-up LP (CAS 1159). *Sympathy* mixes Rare Bird's song with Giazotto's reconstruction of Albinoni's *Adagio*. The version of *Take This Heart* used is live: a studio recording was also made in either 1972 or 1973 but remains unissued.

CAS 1102   DOGGEREL BANK: Mr Skillicorn Dances
1. Where The Sun Always Shines
2. The Man With The Ginger Lily
3. Hyde Park Monster
4. Crazy Lips
5. Lady Jane
6. Oblique Song

1. The Lighthouse Keeper's Bicycle
2. North Circular Blues
3. Cow Pie
4. Sarcophagus Blue
5. Mister Skillicorn Dances
6. Shopping Around
7. Valediction (Rondeau Redouble)

Label: CH4
Rel: Apr 1975[1]
RRP: £2.45[1]

No tape versions notified. This was the last Charisma LP with B&C credits.

The B&C Discography: 1968 to 1975

BCB sequence LP (B&C)

Only one LP issued in the budget–priced series, though B&C/Pegasus material was later issued on the budget Charisma Perspective series. Probably released earlier than indicated below, based on label design, but this particular edition of *Budget Price Records* seems to be the first publication in which release is documented. The June edition listed RRP as 15/6 – there's inflation for you!

BCB 101   BOB AND EARL: Bob And Earl (B&C)

1. Your Time Is My Time (Both)
2. Big Brother (Bob)
3. The Duck (Earl)
4. Baby It's Over (Both)
5. Land Of 1000 Dances (Earl)

1. Puppet On A String (Both)
2. Would You Believe (Earl)
3. My Little Girl (Bob)
4. I'll Keep Running Back (Both)
5. Ooh Honey Baby (Earl)

Label: BC1
Rel: quarter prior to Mar 1970[9]
RRP: 14/6[9]

BCM sequence LPs (B&C)

The BCM mid–priced catalogue sequence outlasted B&C's CAS sequence, with records released long after CAS sequence artists had been transferred to Pegasus. All records listed as stereo in *The New Records* except for BCM 100.

BCM 100   FREDDIE PRIDE: At The Piano (MONO) (B&C)

1. Take The A Train
2. You Go To My Head
3. A Foggy Day
4. Tenderly
5. Tea For Two
6. Blue Moon
7. Caravan

1. I Can't Give You Anything But Love Baby
2. S'Wonderful
3. There Will Never Be Another You
4. Stars Fell On Alabama
5. If I Had You
6. Please Don't Talk About Me When I'm Gone
7. Laura

Label: BC2
Rel: Feb 1970[1]
RRP: 19/11[1]

BCM 101   WILD ANGELS: Live At The Revolution (B&C)

1. Johnny B. Goode
2. Great Balls Of Fire
3. Summertime Blues
4. Jailhouse Rock
5. Say Mama
6. Mean Woman Blues

1. Jeanie Jeanie Jeanie
2. Matchbox
3. Long Tall Sally
4. Cut Across Shorty
5. Rock Around The Clock
6. Whole Lotta Shakin' Goin' On

Label: BC2
Rel: Mar/May '70[1]
RRP: 19/11[1]

Cassette: ZCBCB 101
8–track: Y8BCB 101

Rel: Dec 1972[2]
Rel: Dec 1972[2]

RRP: £1.49[2]
RRP: £1.49[2]

This live album is introduced by Rocking Rosco, who gets a credit under the track listing on the sleeve.

BCM 102   WILD ANGELS: Red Hot 'N' Rockin' (B&C)

1. Little Queenie
2. Stuck On You
3. Somethin' Else
4. Forty Days
5. Odessa
6. Let the Four Winds Blow

1. High School Confidential
2. All Shook Up
3. You Ain't Got Me
4. I Need Your Love Tonight
5. Rave On
6. Bullmoose

Label: BC3
Rel: Nov 1970[1]
RRP: 19/11[1]

Cassette: ZCBCB 102
8–track: Y8BCB 102

Rel: Feb 1973[2]
Rel: Feb 1973[2]

RRP: £1.49[2]
RRP: £1.49[2]

Included a B&C "19/11" price sticker on the sleeve.

The B&C Discography: 1968 to 1975

BCM 103   VARIOUS: Battle Of The Bands (B&C)
1. All By Myself (Shakin' Stevens And The Sunsets)
2. I'm Movin' On (Gene Vincent And The Houseshakers)
3. Lucille (Dave Travis And Bad River)
4. I Don't Wanna Discuss It (Carol Grimes And The Red Price Band)
5. My Babe (Lee Tracy And The Tributes)
6. Lovin' Up a Storm (Memphis Index)

1. Say Mama (Gene Vincent And The Houseshakers)
2. Odessa (Wild Angels)
3. Wee Dock And Doris (Red Price Band)
4. Right Behind You Baby (The Houseshakers)
5. Let the Good Times Roll (Merrill Moore)
6. Lotta Lovin' (Impalas)
7. I'm Walking (Rock And Roll Allstars)

Label: BC3
Rel: Apr/Jun '71[1]
RRP: 99p[1]

Inner sleeve. Shakin' Stevens comes out well on top in this mostly lacklustre battle of the bands!

BCM 104   ROCK 'N' ROLL ALLSTARS: Red China Rocks (B&C)
1. Slippin' And A Sliding
2. Peggy Sue
3. Slow Down
4. Dixie Fried
5. Folsom Prison Blues
6. Blue Suede Shoes
7. 20 Flight Rock

1. Long Tall Sally
2. Rip It Up
3. Bonie Moronie
4. Shakin' All Over
5. It Keeps Raining
6. One Hand Loose
7. My Girl Josephine

Label: BC3
Rel: Jun/Jul '72[1]
RRP: 99p[1]

Cassette: ZCBCB 104
8–track: Y8BCB 104

Rel: Dec 1972[2]
Rel: Dec 1972[2]

RRP: £1.49[2]
RRP: £1.49[2]

BCM 105   VARIOUS: Rock 'N' Roll Party (B&C)
1. My Babe (Lee Tracy)
2. Sally Anne (Wild Angels)
3. Say Mamma (Gene Vincent)
4. Sweet Mama Tree Top Tall (Merrill Moore)
5. Rip It Up (Rock And Roll Allstars)
6. Time To Kill (Wild Angels)
7. Bye Bye Love (Rock And Roll Allstars)
8. Get It On (Rock And Roll Allstars)

1. All By Myself (Shakin' Stevens)
2. I'm Moving On (Gene Vincent)
3. It's Late (Wild Angels)
4. Bonie Maronie (Rock And Roll Allstars)
5. Wrong Number Try Again (Wild Angels)
6. Let The Good Times Roll (Merrill Moore)
7. Three Nights A Week (Wild Angels)
8. It Keeps Raining (Rock And Roll Allstars)
9. Let's Work Together (Rock And Roll Allstars)

Label: BC3
Rel: Dec 1972[1]/ Jan 1973[1]
RRP: 99p[1]

CS/DCS sequence LPs/double LPs (Charisma)

The Charisma Perspective series was introduced in July 1972 as a low–priced budget sequence for compilations and minority–appeal material, including, for no adequately explained reason, other than that B&C and Charisma were, at this point, thick as thieves, material from B&C and Pegasus. Sleeves included a Charisma Perspective sticker and the first three issues included an advertising insert. Two double albums were issued – on these, a "D" preceded the "CS" but they otherwise ran in sequence with the rest of the series. The last in the series was issued in November 1973 shortly after the mid–priced CLASS sequence was introduced in July 1973, which to all intents and purposes replaced the CS series (CLASS was originally intended for live LPs, but soon became the channel for all budget material on Charisma).

The B&C Discography: 1968 to 1975

CS 1   THE NICE: Autumn '67 – Spring '68
1. The Thoughts Of Emerlist Davjack
2. Flower King Of Flies
3. Bonnie K
4. America

1. Diamond Hard Blue Apples Of The Moon
2. Dawn
3. Tantalizin' Maggie
4. The Cry Of Eugene
5. Daddy Where Did I Come From

Label: CH2
Rel: Jul[6]/Aug '72[1]
RRP: £1.49[1]

Cassette: ZCCAB 1
8–track: Y8CAB 1

Rel: Aug 1973[2]
Rel: Aug 1973[2]

RRP: £1.40[2]
RRP: £1.40[2]

Included Charisma Perspective sleeve sticker, "Charisma puts a little colour in your cheeks" advertising inner sleeve plus insert advertising CS 1 to CS 3 and back catalogue by Van der Graaf Generator, Peter Hammill and the Nice. The back catalogue LPs are advertised with a recommended retail price of £2.08. Early Phonogram copies came in original B&C sleeves complete with Charisma Perspective sticker (still priced at £1.49) and Phonogram sticker over the B&C credits.

CS 2   VAN DER GRAAF GENERATOR: 68–71
1. Afterwards
2. Boat Of Millions Of Years
3. Whatever Would Robert Have Said?
4. Lost

1. Necromancer
2. Refugees
3. Darkness
4. Killer

Label: CH2
Rel: Jul[6]/Aug '72[1]
RRP: £1.49[1]

Cassette: ZCCAB 2
8–track: Y8CAB 2

Rel: Aug 1973[2]
Rel: Aug 1973[2]

RRP: £1.40[2]
RRP: £1.40[2]

Included sticker, inner sleeve and insert as per CS 1 above. The version of *Lost* was slightly edited. *Afterwards* and *Necromancer* were licensed from Mercury Records and this represented the first UK issue of these tracks.

CS 3   THE LIVERPOOL SCENE: Recollections
1. The Woo Woo
2. The Day We Danced at the Dole
3. Bat Poem
4. 64
5. Colours
6. I've Got Those Fleetwood Mac, Chicken Shack, John Mayall, Can't Fail Blues

1. Love Is
2. The Entry of Christ into Liverpool
3. Love Story

Label: CH2
Rel: Jul[6]/Aug '72[1]
RRP: £1.49[1]

Cassette: ZCCAB 3
8–track: Y8CAB 3

Rel: Aug 1973[2]
Rel: Aug 1973[2]

RRP: £1.40[2]
RRP: £1.40[2]

Included sticker, inner sleeve and insert as per CS 1 above.

CS 4   THE GROUP: Funny Game, Football...
1. Piraeus Football Club!
2. Crunch!
3. Rangers Abroad
4. An Open Letter to George Best
5. The Missionary
6. Sir Alf Speaks
7. World War III
8. Newsnight with Coleman
9. Soccer Laureate
10. Bovver Boys

1. Scilly Season
2. Government Policies
3. I Remember It Well
4. Floor's the Limit
5. Director's Song
6. Blackbury Town
7. A Joke

Label: CH3
Rel: Sep[6]/Oct '72[1]
RRP: £2.25[1]
Del: Mar 1975[4]

Cassette: ZCCAB 4
8–track: Y8CAB 4

Rel: Aug 1973[2]
Rel: Aug 1973[2]

RRP: £1.40[2]
RRP: £1.40[2]

Sticker and advertising inner sleeve as per CS 1. The majority of issues in the Charisma Perspective series were compilations or records licensed from other record labels (or both). This, however,

The B&C Discography: 1968 to 1975

represents the only issue of completely original material in the series. RRP in *The New Records* is incorrect – this LP retailed at £1.49.

CS 5   STEELEYE SPAN: *Individually And Collectively*

1. The Lark In The Morning (Steeleye Span)
2. Martin Carthy – I Was A Young Man
3. Jigs: Bryan O'Lynn, The Hag With The Money (Steeleye Span)
4. Dancing At Whitsun (Tim Hart)
5. Betsy Bell And Mary Gray (Martin Carthy And Maddy Prior)
6. Female Drummer (Steeleye Span)
7. General Taylor (Steeleye Span)

1. Four Nights Drunk (Steeleye Span)
2. False Knight On The Road (Tim Hart And Maddy Prior)
3. Famous Flower Of Serving Men (Martin Carthy)
4. Three Drunken Maidens (Tim Hart And Maddy Prior)
5. When I Was On Horseback (Steeleye Span)

Label: CH3
Rel: Oct[6]/Nov '72[1]
RRP: £2.25[1]

Cassette: ZCCAB 5   Rel: Aug 1973[2]   RRP: £1.40[2]
8–track: Y8CAB 5   Rel: Aug 1973[2]   RRP: £1.40[2]

Sticker and advertising inner sleeve as per CS 1. RRP in *The New Records* is incorrect – this LP retailed at £1.49.

CS 6   ANDY ROBERTS: *Andy Roberts*

1. Midnight Shift
2. Percy Parslow's Hamster Farm
3. Radio Lady
4. Burdock River Run
5. Moths And Lizards In Detroit

1. Sitting On A Rock
2. Keep My Children Warm
3. Homegrown
4. The Raven
5. Goodtime Charlie

Label: CH3
Rel: Jan[6]/Feb '73[1]
RRP: £1.49[1]

Cassette: ZCCAB 6   Rel: Aug 1973[2]   RRP: £1.40[2]
8–track: Y8CAB 6   Rel: Aug 1973[2]   RRP: £1.40[2]

This comprised solo material plus tracks from the Liverpool Scene and the Everyone LP.

CS 7   AUDIENCE: *You Can't Beat 'Em*

1. Trombone Gulch
2. Thunder And Lightnin'
3. Raviole
4. Elixir Of Youth
5. I Had A Dream
6. You're Not Smiling

1. Ain't The Man You Need
2. It Brings A Tear
3. Indian Summer
4. Jackdaw
5. Nancy

Label: CH3
Rel: Jan[6]/Feb '73[1]
RRP: £1.49[1]

Cassette: ZCCAB 7   Rel: Aug 1973[2]   RRP: £1.40[2]
8–track: Y8CAB 7   Rel: Aug 1973[2]   RRP: £1.40[2]

Sticker as per CS1. Included the otherwise unreleased track, *Elixir of Youth*.

CS 8   THE CREATION: *The Creation '66 – '67*

1. Making Time
2. Life Is Just Beginning
3. If I Stay Too Long
4. Through My Eyes
5. Hey Joe
6. Painter Man

1. Cool Jerk
2. How Does It Feel
3. Try And Stop Me
4. I Am The Walker
5. Can I Join Your Band
6. Tom Tom

Label: CH3
Rel: Jul[6]/Aug '73[1]
RRP: £1.43[1]

Cassette: ZCCAB 8   Rel: Nov 1973[2]   RRP: £1.40[2]
8–track: Y8CAB 8   Rel: Nov 1973[2]   RRP: £1.40[2]

RRP in *The New Records* is incorrect – this LP retailed at £1.49.

The B&C Discography: 1968 to 1975

CS 9   ATOMIC ROOSTER: Assortment
1. Devil's Answer
2. Sleeping For Years
3. Friday The 13th
4. I Can't Take No More
5. Death Walks Behind You

1. Tomorrow Night
2. Break The Ice
3. S.L.Y.
4. The Price
5. Decline And Fall

Label: CH3
Rel: Aug[6]/Sep'73[1]
RRP: £1.43[1]

Cassette: ZCCAB 9
8-track: Y8CAB 9
RRP in *The New Records* is incorrect – this LP retailed at £1.49.

Rel: Nov 1973[2]
Rel: Nov 1973[2]

RRP: £1.40[2]
RRP: £1.40[2]

DCS 10 ORSON WELLES: The War Of The Worlds (2–LP)
No specific track listing.

Label: CH3
Rel: Aug[6]/Sep'73[1]
RRP: £2.49[1]

Cassette: ZCCBD 10
8-track: Y8CBD 10

Rel: Mar 1974[2]
Rel: Mar 1974[2]

RRP: £3.20[2]
RRP: £3.20[2]

This was the first of two double albums in the Charisma Perspective series, hence the addition of a "D" to the catalogue number. Set part numbers are as follows: record one is DC 1; record two is DC 2. The "DC" set part numbers appear in the run–off groove with a few amendments to matrix numbers to take into account that side 1 is coupled with side 3 and side 2 is coupled with side 4. The labels credit Orson Welles with the sub–credit, "Radioplay by Howard Koch" and state a 1969 publication date. The sleeve includes the following information: "The original broadcast that panicked the nation!...The actual broadcast by The Mercury Theatre on the Air as heard over the Columbia Broadcasting System, Oct 30, 1938. The most thrilling drama ever broadcast from the famed HOWARD KOCH script!"

Cassette version most likely issued on a single cassette, whilst the 8–track version was most likely issued as two separate cartridges. See DCS 11 below for further information on tape releases.

DCS 11 VARIOUS: The Golden Age Of Comedy Volume One (2–LP)

Side 1:
1. Eddie Cantor (With Bert Gordon "The Mad Russian")
2. Fibber McGee And Molly (Jim And Marion Jordan)
3. Bud Abbott And Lou Costello
4. Fred Allen – Jack Benny "Feud"
5. Jackie Gleason

Side 3:
1. Red Skelton
2. Oscar Levant (With Fred Allen)
3. Baron Munchausen
4. Bob And Ray
5. Fred Allen (With Tallulah Bankhead)

Label: CH3
Rel: Aug[6]/Sep'73[1]
RRP: £2.49[1]

Side 2:
1. Sid Ceasar – Imogen Coca
2. George Burns And Gracie Allen
3. Groucho Marx
4. Ernie Kovacs
5. Milton Berle

Side 4:
1. George Jessel
2. Ed Wynn
3. Jack Benny
4. Smith And Dale
5. Laurel And Hardy

Cassette: ZCCBD 11
8-track: Y8CBD 11

Rel: Nov 1973[2]
Rel: Nov 1973[2]

RRP: £2.45[2]
RRP: £2.45[2]

Set part numbers are as follows: record one is DC 3; record two is DC 4. The "DC" set part numbers appear in the run–off groove. The labels state a 1972 publication date and despite the optimism of the title there was no *Volume Two*.

The New Cassettes credits the cassette version as "Double play", which suggests that it was issued on a single cassette (the 8–track version was issued as two separate cartridges). The cassette version also appears in the March 1974 edition of *The New Cassettes* with a price of £3.29.

CS 12   STEELEYE SPAN: Almanac

1. The Hills Of Greenmore
2. My Johnnie Was A Shoemaker
3. The Wee Weaver
4. Reels
5. False Knight On The Road
6. Lowlands Of Holland

1. All Things Are Quite Silent
2. Jigs
3. Prince Charlie Stewart
4. Gower Wassail
5. Skewball

Label: CH3
Rel: Sep[1]/Nov '73[6]
RRP: £1.43[1]

RRP in *The New Records* is incorrect – this LP retailed at £1.49. Included a selection of tracks from the B&C and Pegasus Steeleye Span albums, plus *All Things Are Now Silent, Lowlands Of Holland*, and *The Hills Of Greenmore* from the first Steeleye Span LP, *Hark, The Village Wait*, SF 8113, issued on RCA Victor in 1970. No tape versions notified.

CLASS sequence LPs (Charisma)

This mid–price budget series was introduced in July 1973 with *Genesis Live* and *Lindisfarne Live*, which were marketed as "Charisma Live Giants". However, the sequence soon took over from the low price Charisma Perspective budget series for the issue of various artists compilations as well.

CLASS 1   GENESIS: Genesis Live

1. Watcher Of The Skies
2. Get 'Em Out By Friday
3. The Return Of The Giant Hogweed

1. Musical Box
2. The Knife

Label: CH3
Rel: Jul[6]/Aug '73[1]
RRP: £1.99[1]

Cassette: ZCCAS 1
8–track: Y8CAS 1

Rel: Sep 1973[2]
Rel: Sep 1973[2]

RRP: £2.35[2]
RRP: £2.35[2]

Some include a "Charisma Live Giants" sticker. February 1973 concerts originally recorded for the US radio show, *The King Biscuit Hour*.

CLASS 2   LINDISFARNE: Lindisfarne Live

1. No Time To Lose
2. Meet Me On The Corner
3. Alright On The Night
4. Train In G. Major
5. Fog On The Tyne

1. We Can Swing Together
2. Jack Hammer Blues

Label: CH3
Rel: Jul[6]/Aug '73[1]
RRP: £1.99[1]

Cassette: ZCCAS 2
8–track: Y8CAS 2

Rel: Sep 1973[2]
Rel: Sep 1973[2]

RRP: £2.35[2]
RRP: £2.35[2]

CLASS 3   VARIOUS: One More Chance

1. Indian Summer (Audience)
2. Eric The Half A Bee (Monty Python)
3. Happy The Man (Genesis)
4. Wherewithal (Clifford T. Ward)
5. Wake Up Little Sister
    (Capability Brown)
6. Orang Outang (Jo'Burg Hawk)
7. Numbers (Alan Hull)
8. She Belongs To Me (Graham Bell
    With Arc)

1. Theme One (Van Der
    Graaf Generator)
2. One More Dance (Jack The Lad)
3. Country Pie (The Nice)
4. What You Want To Know (Rare Bird)
5. It's A Game (String Drive Thing)
6. Clear White Light (Lindisfarne)

Label: CH4
Rel: May[6]/Jun '74[1]
RRP: £1.99[1]

Inner sleeve. Compilation of various single a–sides, most often sought after because it is the cheapest way to get a copy of *Happy the Man* by Genesis on UK vinyl, especially because it has now been confirmed that this is a different version to the single issue (CB 181). No tape versions notified.

The B&C Discography: 1968 to 1975

CLASS 4   **MONTY PYTHON: Live At Drury Lane**

1. Introduction	1. Spot The Brain Cell	Label: CH4
2. Llamas	2. Bruces	Rel: Jul[6]/Aug '74[1]
3. Gumby – Flower Arranging	3. Argument	RRP: £1.99[1]
4. Secret Service	4. Four Yorkshiremen	
5. Wrestling	5. Election Special	
6. Communist Quiz	6. Lumberjack Song	
7. Idiot Song	7. Parrot Sketch	
8. Albatross		
9. Colonel		
10. Nudge, Nudge		
11. Cocktail Bar		
12. Travel Agent		

Cassette: ZCCAS 4   Rel: Jul 1974[2]   RRP: £2.45[2]
8–track: Y8CAS 4   Rel: Jul 1974[2]   RRP: £2.45[2]

Early copies with full B&C label text have rough textured labels. Later copies with B&C marketing text have smooth labels, though with pronounced roughness in the centre. B&C copies have sleeve credit, "Made & Printed by Bruin B. V., Zaandam – Holland". The reason was that the ladies in EMI's pressing department refused to press the album because of the amount and variety of swearing. Original copies have one of Porky's messages on side 2, "The wonderful world of Porky Trishy Melly yeah". Promotional stickers were foot-shaped and stated, "NEW ALBUM ON CHARISMA – MONTY PYTHON AT DRURY LANE – CLASS 4".

CLASS 5   **VARIOUS: Charisma Keyboards**

1. America (The Nice)	1. As Your Mind Flies By (Rare Bird)	Label: see below
2. The Fountain Of Salmacis (Genesis)	2. White Hammer (Van Der Graaf Generator)	Rel: Jul[6]/Aug '74[1]
3. Mountains (Robert John Godfrey)	3. Flight To The Ford (Bo Hansson)	RRP: £1.99[1]

Cassette: ZCCAS 5   Rel: Sep 1974[2]   RRP: £2.40[2]
8–track: Y8CAS 5   Rel: Sep 1974[2]   RRP: £2.40[2]

Inner sleeve. CH5 label design confirmed, but must exist on CH4 if the release date is correct, which would appear to be the case. The matrix on side 1 has "B" crossed out and replaced by "A" and side 2 has "A" crossed out and replaced by "B". Either they got the matrix numbers the wrong way around or they changed their minds. The Bo Hansson track comprises two segued tracks, *The Black Riders* and *Flight to the Ford*. On *America* you can hear a few seconds of audience participation that were not included on the original release on *Elegy* (CAS 1030).

CADS sequence double LP (Charisma)

CADS 101   **VARIOUS: Music From Free Creek**

Side 1:	Side 3:	
1. Cissy Strutt	1. Getting Back to Molly	Label: CH3
2. Freedom Jazz Dance	2. Cherry Picker	Rel: Jun 1973[6]
3. Sympathy For The Devil	3. Kilpartrick's Defeat	RRP: £3.49
4. Mother Nature's Son	4. The Girl From Ipanema	
5. Road Song	5. No One Knows	

Side 2:	Side 4:
1. Lay Lady Lay	1. Living Like A Fool
2. Hey Jude	2. Working In The Coalmine
3. He Darked The Sun	3. Big City Woman
4. Earle's Shuffle	4. On the Rebound

Cassette: ZCCAD 101   Rel: Jun 1973[2]   RRP: £3.20[2]
8–track: Y8CAD 101   Rel: Jun 1973[2]   RRP: £3.20[2]

The B&C Discography: 1968 to 1975

Original copies included a £3.49 custom price sticker. Set part numbers are ADS 1 and ADS 2, which appear in the run–off. Some copies seem to have been pressed in Holland for the UK market, in that Dutch copies with UK B&C credits exist. Two pseudonyms were used because of copyright issues: "King Cool" and "A. N. Other" were Eric Clapton and Jeff Beck respectively. This was recorded and mixed at New York City's Record Plant during June, July and Aug 1969 and most the album was made up of recordings from four specific sets of sessions as follows:

The Eric Clapton Session: No One Knows, Road Song and Getting Back To Molly.
The Jeff Beck Session: Cissy Strut, Big City Woman, Cherrypicker and Working In A Coalmine.
The Keith Emerson Session: Freedom Jazz Dance, On The Rebound and Mother Nature's Son.
The Harvey Mandel Session: Sympathy Jam and Earl's Shuffle.

The New Cassettes credits the cassette version as "Double play", which suggests that it was issued on a single cassette. The 8–track version was probably issued on two cartridges.

TSS sequence double LP (Charisma)

For anyone wondering why *Charisma Disturbance* was assigned "TSS 1", the letters stand for "Tony Stratton Smith" and the LP was issued to commemorate Charisma's 4th anniversary in November 1973. This said then, it remains a bit of a mystery as to why EMI decided to celebrate Charisma's 25th anniversary in 2003, a whole year early.

TSS 1   **VARIOUS:** *Charisma Disturbance*

Side 1:
1. Sonato Pian E Forte (Sinfonia Of London Conducted By Joseph Eger)
2. The Unanswered Question (John Neville)
3. Intermezzo 'Karelia Suite' (The Nice)
4. German Overalls (Peter Hammill)

Side 2:
1. Money Game (Alan Hull)
2. She Belongs To Me (Bell And Arc)
3. Spam Song (Monty Python)
4. Lady Eleanor (Lindisfarne)
5. Flight To The Ford (Bo Hansson)
6. Fog On The Tyne (Lindisfarne)

Side 3:
1. No Range (Capability Brown)
2. Sympathy (Rare Bird)
3. I Had A Dream (Audience)
4. Home Thoughts From Abroad (Clifford T. Ward)
5. Killer (Van Der Graaf Generator)

Side 4:
1. Getting Back To Molly (Music From Free Creek)
2. Too Many People (Graham Bell)
3. Dark Side Of The Moon (Jo'burg Hawk)
4. Regent Street Incident (String Driven Thing)
5. Return Of The Giant Hogweed (Genesis)

Label: CH3
Rel: Nov[6]/Dec'73[1]
RRP: £1.99[1]

Cassette: ZCCBD 100   **Rel:** Dec 1973[2]   **RRP:** £2.45[2]
8–track: Y8CBD 100   **Rel:** Dec 1973[2]   **RRP:** £2.45[2]

2-LP set in top-opening die-cut, fold-open single sleeve with die-cut inner sleeves – the die-cut centres were on one side only. Set part numbers are TS. 101 and TS. 102, which appear in the run–offs and the inner sleeves. Track listing above taken from sleeve; differences in label credits are as follows. *Sonato Pian E Forte* is credited to "Joseph Eger with the Sinfonia of London", *The Unanswered Question* to "The Sinfonia of London Conducted by Joseph Eger, words spoken by John Neville" and *Intermezzo 'Karelia Suite'* to "The Nice and the Sinfonia of London Conducted by Joseph Eger". Bo Hansson's track comprises two segued tracks, *The Black Riders* and *Flight to the Ford.*

The New Cassettes credits the cassette version as "Double play", which suggests that it was issued on a single cassette. The 8–track version was probably issued on two cartridges.

CGS sequence double LPs (Charisma)

The short–run CGS sequence was first used for the Genesis double LP, *The Lamb Lies Down On Broadway*, and was then used for two boxed sets each comprising of two back catalogue single Genesis LPs plus poster.

CGS 101   GENESIS: The Lamb Lies Down On Broadway

Side 1:
1. The Lamb Lies Down On Broadway
2. Fly On A Windshield
3. Broadway Melody Of 1974
4. Cuckoo Cocoon
5. In The Cage
6. The Grand Parade Of
    Lifeless Packaging

Side 2:
1. Back in N.Y.C.
2. Hairless Heart
3. Counting Out Time
4. Carpet Crawl
5. The Chamber Of 32 Doors

Side 3:
1. Lilywhite Lilith
2. The Waiting Room
3. Anyway
4. Here Comes The
    Supernatural Anaesthetist
5. The Lamia
6. Silent Sorrow In Empty Boats

Side 4:
1. The Colony Of Slippermen:
2. Arrival
3. A Visit to the Doktor
4. Raven
5. Ravine
6. The Light Dies Down On Broadway
7. Riding The Scree
8. In The Rapids
9. It

Label: see below
Rel: Nov[6]/Dec'74[1]
RRP: £4.49[1]

Cassette: ZCCGS 101   Rel: Dec 1974[2]   RRP: £4.49[2]
8–track: Y8CGS 101   Rel: Dec 1974[2]   RRP: £4.49[2]

Inner sleeves. Set part numbers are CG 1 and CG 2. The part numbers appear in the run–off groove. The side–two labels were of custom design, whilst the original press has the CH5 label design. This is a difficult album to find in both original form and perfect condition and there is confusion as to what represents an original copy. Most collectors search for copies on the CH4 label design with the full "Manufactured and distributed by B&C..." text, assuming that this represents an original copy. However, it is certain that the original pressing is the CH5 label design with the "Marketed by B&C..." text and a 'Printed and Made by Bruin B. V. Zaandam/Holland' credit on the sleeve. CH4 copies represent pressings from early 1975 when Charisma seems to have been using up old label blanks.

Just to make things more difficult, record one of the original pressing is said to have suffered from pressing faults and many copies were returned several times. Certainly, this would explain why there are numerous copies with a mix of CH4 and CH5 labels, and even some with one B&C label of either type and one Phonogram credited label. The sleeve with both B&C and Bruin credits continued to be used for the first batch of Phonogram–manufactured records. It is amusing to note that, because the original B&C credit was well hidden in the reams of sleeve notes, Phonogram copies continued to include this credit throughout the rest of the 1970s and into the 1980s.

Memory says that the cassette version was issued as two separate cassettes (I could be wrong). 8–track version issued as two separate cartridges, both with outer sleeves, in an overall box.

CGS 102   GENESIS: The Genesis Collection, Vol. 1
CGS 103   GENESIS: The Genesis Collection, Vol. 2
See below for track listing information

Label: see below
Rel: Apr 1975[12]
RRP: £4.49[12]

Both sets issued in a top–opening, fold–open sleeve with poster – posters were of different design in each set. CGS 102 comprised *Trespass* and *Nursery Chryme* (see CAS 1020 and CAS 1052 for track listing) and CGS 103 comprised *Foxtrot* and *Selling England By The Pound* (see CAS 1058 and CAS 1074 for track listing). All LPs came in their normal sleeves. The only verified original copy of CGS

102 viewed has both LPs on the CH3 label design. However, two verified original copies of CGS 103 have label and sleeve variations. In one, *Foxtrot* has a textured sleeve and both records have the CH5 label design. In the other, *Foxtrot* is in a non-textured sleeve and has the CH4 label design. Sadly, *Selling England* was missing from this other set. By the look of things, this would tend to suggest that Charisma was either using up old label blanks or were using up unsold stock. Your guess is as good as mine. It is likely that other sleeve/label variations exist. No tape versions available.

Both sets were available between April and June 1975, but became rarer than intended because many record dealers threw away the box sleeve and sold the separate LPs at the normal price, thus making an extra 41p per set. Some dealers are rumoured to have sold the posters separately, and others randomly shoved the poster into one or other of the sleeves after disposing of the outer box.

CB sequence 7" singles (B&C and Charisma)

Charisma singles were issued on B&C's pre-existing CB catalogue number sequence – the first Charisma release was Topo D. Bil's *Witchi–Tai–To* (CB 116), released the week of 23 January 1970 and the last B&C label record was Jawbone's *Gotta Go* (CB 190) in August 1972. From this point the sequence was used exclusively by Charisma until 1987, when that label was absorbed into Virgin. After B&C ceased to use the sequence many, but not all, releases were pressed up with the same track on both sides for promotional use. Where different (and known) this is noted.

CB 100   MERRILL MOORE: *Sweet Mama Tree Top Tall / Little Green Apples (B&C)*
Label: BC1   Rel: 2 May 1969[3]

CB 101   JAMES CARR: *Freedom Train / That's The Way Love Turned Out For Me (B&C)*
Label: BC1   Rel: 2 May 1969[3]
Promotional copies exist with "D.J. copy not for resale" on the label.

CB 102   BOB AND EARL: *Dancin' Everywhere / Baby It's Over (B&C)*
Label: BC1   Rel: 16 May or 23 May 1969[3]

CB 103   THE KENTUCKIANS: *Pop–A–Top / How'd We Ever Get This Way (B&C)*
Label: BC1   Rel: 13 Jun or 20th Jun 1969[3]

CB 104   HORACE FAITH: *Spinning Wheel / Like I Used To Do (B&C)*
Label: BC1   Rel: 13 Jun or 20 Jun 1969[3]
The b-side matrix is "CB 102", corrected by hand to replace the "2" with a "4".

CB 105   JACKIE LEE AND DELORES HALL: *Whether It's Right Or Wrong / Baby I'm Satisfied (B&C)*
Label: BC2   Rel: 25 Jul or 1 Aug 1969[3]
Originally intended for issue on the Action label ("ACT+4544+A"/"ACT+4544+B" crossed out in the run–off). Promotional copies with large "A" on label. Jackie Lee was a pseudonym for Earl Nelson, of Bob and Earl. *Baby I'm Satisfied* originally issued on Sue (WI 393) in 1965, credited to Bob and Earl.

CB 106   CLYDE McPHATTER: *Denver / Tell Me (B&C)*
Label: BC2   Rel: 6 Oct 1969[3]

CB 107   AARON NEVILLE: *Tell It Like It Is / Why Worry (B&C)*
Label: BC2   Rel: 22 Aug 1969[3]
Originally issued on Stateside as SS 584 in 1967. *Record Retailer* has a release date of 8 August.

The B&C Discography: 1968 to 1975

CB 108   *NO RELEASE (INTENDED FOR B&C RELEASE)*
The B&C/Action/Stable catalogue for 1970 confirms no release on this catalogue number. A 1980 pirate press of *The Ching–A–Ling Song / Supermen* was issued in picture sleeve as CB 108, credited to "Feathers", but with a very unconvincing B&C label design. Feathers included a young Bowie.

CB 109   *NO RELEASE (INTENDED FOR B&C RELEASE)*
The B&C/Action/Stable catalogue for 1970 confirms no release on this catalogue number.

CB 110   *DON FOX: Once In A While / You Belong To My Heart (B&C)*
Label: BC2   Rel: 3 Oct 1969[3]

CB 111   *SIMON K: You Know I Do / Bring Your Love Back (B&C)*
Label: BC2   Rel: 5 Dec 1969[3]

CB 112   *THE HOUSE OF LORDS: In The Land Of Dreams / Ain't Gonna Wait Forever (B&C)*
Label: BC2   Rel: 24 Oct 1969[3]

CB 113   *GINGERBREAD: How Are You / Easy Girl (B&C)*
Label: BC2   Rel: 31 Oct 1969[3]
DJ copies exist with "DJ COPY" and small "A" on the label.

CB 114   *WILD ANGELS: Buzz Buzz / Please Don't Touch (B&C)*
Label: BC2   Rel: 21 Nov 1969[3]

CB 115   *DRY ICE: Running To The Convent / Nowhere To Go (B&C)*
Label: BC2   Rel: 5 Dec 1969[3]

CB 116   *TOPO D. BIL: Witchi–Tai–To / Jam*
Label: CH1   Rel: 23 Jan 1970[3]
Picture sleeve. Some picture sleeves include an incorrect "CB 114" catalogue number with misspelled track credit, "Wichi–Tai–To" (i.e. missing out the "t" in the first word).

CB 117   *JILL DAY: I'll Think About You / The Way of Love (B&C)*
Label: BC2   Rel: 1 May 1970[3]

CB 118   *RICHARD TURNER: Serenade To Summertime / Starshine (B&C: NOT RELEASED)*
CB 118   *THE JOHNNY ARTHEY ORCHESTRA: Serenade To The Summer / Star Shine (B&C)*
Label: BC2   Rel: 6 Mar 1970[3]
First listed in *The New Singles* for 13 February 1970 credited to Richard Turner, whoever he was – perhaps the backing track sounded better without the singer and they wiped the vocal track. Who knows? The March notification in *The New Singles* (i.e. the released version) credits the titles as per the February listing (though now with correct artist). Picture sleeve credits b–side as "Star's Shine".

CB 119   *THE FORUM: The River Is Wide / I Fall In Love All Over Again (B&C)*
Label: BC2   Rel: 6 Feb 1970[3]
Originally issued on London as HLM 10120 in 1967.

CB 120   *RARE BIRD: Sympathy / Devil's High Concern*
Label: CH1   Rel: 6 Feb 1970[3] (del: 1973 (MMSC3)
Most copies are Orlake pressings, though three–pronged Philips–pressed copies are also confirmed.

The B&C Discography: 1968 to 1975

CB 121   **ATOMIC ROOSTER: Friday The Thirteenth / Banstead (B&C)**
Label: BC1   Rel: 13 Mar 1970[3]
Picture sleeve credits "Friday the 13th" whilst label credits "Friday the Thirteenth".

CB 122   **VAN DER GRAAF GENERATOR: Refugees / The Boat Of A Million Years**
Label: CH1   Rel: 17 Apr 1970[3]
Three-prong Philips press. The a-side is a different version to that on CAS 1007.

CB 123   **WILD ANGELS: Sally Ann / Wrong Number, Try Again (B&C)**
Label: BC2   Rel: 5 Jun 1970[3]

CB 124   **BENNETT AND EVANS: No, No You Don't Know / The Path Is Hard To Follow (B&C)**
Label: BC2   Rel: 26 Jun 1970[3]

CB 125   **FREDDIE NOTES AND THE RUDIES: It Came Out Of The Sky / Well Oh Well (B&C)**
Label: BC2   Rel: 17 Apr 1970[3]
Picture sleeve.

CB 126   **AUDIENCE: Belladonna Moonshine / The Big Spell**
Label: CH1   Rel: 26 Jun 1970[3]
Solid-centred Orlake pressings and Philips pressings with large centre-hole exist.

CB 127   **SWEET SALVATION: Honey Man / Freedom City (B&C)**
Label: BC2   Rel: 10 Jul 1970[3]
A-side reissued in Jan 1971 on CB 139 with new b-side. *Honey Man* was co-composed by Cat Stevens and was supposedly to be recorded with Elton John, though this plan fell through.

CB 128   **RAY MORGAN: Long And Winding Road / The Sweetest Wine (B&C)**
Label: BC2   Rel: 3 Jul 1970[3]/19 Oct 1973[3]
Second trade listing suggests plenty of copies still in stock at B&C's Music House warehouse in 1973!

CB 129   **CAROL GRIMES AND DELIVERY: Harry Lucky / Homemade Ruin (B&C)**
Label: BC2   Rel: 28 Aug 1970[3]
Probably the first single pressing under the contract with EMI.

CB 130   **TREVOR BILLMUSS: Whoops Amour / Sunday Afternoon In Belgrave Square**
Label: CH1   Rel: 25 Sep 1970[3]

CB 131   **ATOMIC ROOSTER: Tomorrow Night / Play The Game (B&C)**
Label: BC2   Rel: 25 Sep 1970[3]
White label test pressings exist.

CB 132   **THE NICE: Country Pie / One Of Those People**
Label: CH1   Rel: 6 Nov 1970[3]

CB 133   **FRIENDSHIP: The World Is Going To Be A Better Place / A Million Hearts (B&C)**
Label: BC2   Rel: 6 Nov 1970[3]

The B&C Discography: 1968 to 1975

CB 134   *LEWIS RICH: The Prophet / Freedom City (B&C)*
Label: BC2   Rel: 20 Nov 1970[3]
Promotional picture sleeve says "The record sleeve ... is promotional only and will not be used in the general distribution to the record." It was then issued in the picture sleeve with above text removed!

CB 135   *RAY MORGAN: Barefoot Days / Love Doesn't Change (B&C)*
Label: BC2   Rel: 20 Nov 1970[3]

CB 136   *SWEET SALVATION: Honey Man / The Crucifix, Swastika And Star (B&C)*
Label: BC2   Rel: 29 Jan or 5 Feb 1971[3]
A-side previously issued on CB 127 with different b-side.

CB 137   *LINDISFARNE: Clear White Light – Part 2 / Knacker's Yard Blues*
Label: CH1   Rel: 20 Nov 1970[3]

CB 138   *RARE BIRD: What You Want To Know / Hammerhead*
Label: CH1   Rel: 27 Nov 1970[3]
A-side seems to be a remixed version of the track from CAS 1011 with more prominent cymbals.

CB 139   *THE WEATHERMEN: It's The Same Old Song / Why Should I Fight (B&C)*
Label: BC2   Rel: 11 Dec 1970[3]

CB 140   *RAY MORGAN: No More Tears / Wheel Keeps Turning (B&C)*
Label: BC2   Rel: 29 Jan or 5 Feb 1971[3]

CB 141   *AUDIENCE: Indian Summer / It Brings A Tear (DJ COPY)*
CB 141   *AUDIENCE: Indian Summer / It Brings A Tear / Priestess*
Label: CH2   Rel: 19 Feb[8]/26 Mar 1971[3]
Picture sleeve. Two tracks on a-side. Different (and better) version of *Priestess* to that on the album. The DJ lables include February release date and matrix numbers ("CB. 141A/2U"/"CB. 141A/3U").

CB 142   *REDWOOD: Didn't I (Blow Your Mind) / Homemade Happy Day (B&C)*
Label: BC2   Rel: 12 Feb 1971[3]
Exists with both solid and 4-prong die-cut centres.

CB 143   *NO RELEASE (PRESUMABLY INTENDED FOR B&C RELEASE)*

CB 144   *NO RELEASE (PRESUMABLY INTENDED FOR B&C RELEASE)*

CB 145   *WILD ANGELS: Three Nights A Week / Time To Kill (B&C)*
Label: BC2   Rel: 2 Apr 1971[3]

CB 146   *EVERYONE: Trouble At The Mill / Radio Lady (B&C)*
Label: BC2   Rel: 2 Apr 1971[3]

CB 147   *THE WEATHERMEN: Honey Bee (Keep On Stinging Me) / Anarchy Rock) (B&C)*
Label: BC2   Rel: 9 Apr 1971[3]

CB 148   *EMPEROR ROSKO: Customs Man / Take It In Your Stride (B&C)*
Label: BC2   Rel: 16 Apr 1971[3]

The B&C Discography: 1968 to 1975

CB 149   **THE ARNOLD CORNS: Moonage Daydream / Hang On To Yourself (B&C)**
Label: BC2   Rel: 23 Apr 1971[3]

CB 150   **RAY MORGAN: Let's Fall In Love Again / The Path Is Hard To Follow (B&C)**
Label: BC2   Rel: 21 May 1971[3]

CB 151   **BITCH: Laughing / House Where I Live (B&C)**
Label: BC2   Rel: 21 May[3]/11 Jun 1971[3]
The New Singles for 11 June miscredits the band as "Hitch".

CB 152   **GENESIS: The Knife / The Knife (Part 2)**
Label: CH2   Rel: 21 May 1971[3]
Picture sleeve shows the then new line-up rather than the line-up that plays on the record.

CB 153   **LINDISFARNE: Lady Eleanor / Nothing But The Marvellous Is Beautiful**
Label: CH2   Rel: 21 May 1971[3]
Most 4-prong and solid centre A2U/B2U copies have a "From the L.P. CAS 1025 – "Nicely Out Of Tune"" credit though some A2U/B2U (and A3U/B2U) copies do not. A1U/B1U and A3U/B2U copies confirmed in picture sleeve. Two different versions ("Music playing in my bone" and "Music playing in my bones"). Original handwritten lyrics by Alan Hull titled "Lady Elenore (Nightmare Festival)".

CB 154   **THE HERD: You've Got Me Hanging From Your Lovin' Tree / I Don't Wanna Go To Sleep Again (B&C)**
Label: BC2   Rel: 4 Jun 1971[3]

CB 155   **ROCK AND ROLL ALLSTARS: Baby Can You Feel It / It Keeps Raining (B&C)**
Label: BC2   Rel: 28 May[3]/18 Jun 1971[3]

CB 156   **AUDIENCE: Raviole / Eye To Eye (NOT RELEASED)**
CB 156   **AUDIENCE: Eye To Eye / Eye To Eye (MISPRESS? PROMO?)**
CB 156   **AUDIENCE: You're Not Smiling / Eye To Eye**
Label: CH2   Rel: 16 Jul 1971[3] (as released)
The New Singles lists "Raviole" for release on 28 May 1971. Copies then appeared with the b-side on both sides. Next up was a promotional pressing (BCP 1) with changed a-side. The release in July was with tracks as per BCP 1. Some copies exist with a very large "A" hand stamped on the b-side.

CB 157   **ATOMIC ROOSTER: Devil's Answer / The Rock (B&C)**
Label: BC2   Rel: 28 May 1971[3]
A 7" pressing on a 12" acetate plate exists with credits written in what looks like chalk.

CB 158   **TREVOR BILLMUSS: English Pastures / Fishing Songs (B&C)**
Label: BC2   Rel: 18 Jun 1971[3]
The b-side is taken from the Charisma LP (CAS 1017), where it is titled "Fishing Song".

CB 159   **GARY CHARLES: You've Been Away Too Long / Lovely Linda (B&C)**
Label: BC2   Rel: 16 Jul 1971[3]

CB 160   **JO TAYLOR: The Junkman's Serenade / You Fooled Me (B&C)**
Label: BC2   Rel: 30 Jul 1971[3]

The B&C Discography: 1968 to 1975

CB 161   MARC ELLINGTON: *Alligator Man / Song For A Friend* (B&C)
Label: BC2   Rel: 30 Jul 1971[3]

CB 162   THE WEATHERMEN: *Fine Together Stomp / Fred Parsons, Jim Flynn, Waxie Maxie, Lee Gopthal, Old Uncle Clive Crawley And All* (B&C)
Label: BC2   Rel: 27 Aug 1971[3]

CB 163   FRIENDSHIP: *Stop Living Alone / Friends Make Living What It Is* (B&C)
Label: BC2   Rel: 24 Sep 1971[3]

CB 164   STEELEYE SPAN: *Rave On / Reels / Female Drummer* (B&C)
Label: BC2   Rel: 1 Oct 1971[3]
Picture sleeve.

CB 165   PAUL KENT: *Do You / Helpless Harry* (B&C)
Label: BC2   Rel: 29 Oct 1971[3]

CB 166   MOTHER NATURE: *Orange Days And Purple Nights / Where Did She Go* (B&C)
Label: BC2   Rel: 1 Oct[3]/5th Nov 1971[3]

CB 167   RAY MORGAN: *Friend, Lover, Woman, Wife / Burning Bridges* (B&C)
Label: BC2   Rel: 5 Nov 1971[3]

CB 168   JAW BONE JUG BAND: *Jailhouse Rock / Jugband Music* (B&C)
Label: BC2   Rel: 19 Nov 1971[3]

CB 169   WISHFUL THINKING: *Lu La Le Lu / We're Gonna Change All This* (B&C)
Label: BC2   Rel: 4 Feb 1972[3]

CB 170   BELL AND ARC: *She Belongs To Me / Dawn*
Label: CH2   Rel: 3 Dec 1971[3]

CB 171   ROCK AND ROLL ALLSTARS: *Rock And Roll Allstars Play Party Rock: Boney Moroney/Get It On/Rip It Up / Rock And Roll Allstars Play Party Rock: Let's Work Together/It Keeps Raining/Bye Bye Love* (B&C)
Label: BC2   Rel: 17 Dec 1971[3]
Medleys with dubbed applause. Mistakenly listed in *The New Records* with LP list price of £2.05.

CB 172   JIMMY JUSTICE: *English Rose / Burgandy, Port And Red Wine* (B&C)
Label: BC2   Rel: 7th Jan[8]/21 Jan 1972[3]
Promotional copies with 4–prong centre exist.

CB 173   LINDISFARNE: *Meet Me On The Corner / Scotch Mist / No Time To Lose*
Label: CH2   Rel: 14 Jan[3]/11 Feb 1972[3]
Original picture sleeve advertises only *Fog On The Tyne* on rear; second adds *Nicely Out Of Tune*.

The B&C Discography: 1968 to 1975

CB 174 GARY CHARLES: Love Into My Life / When You Run Out Of Breath (B&C)
Label: BC2 Rel: 11 Feb 1972[3]

CB 175 VAN DER GRAAF GENERATOR: Theme One / W
Label: CH2 Rel: 4 Feb 1972[3]
Solid centre copies with picture sleeve confirmed. Whether 4-prong copies were also issued with picture sleeve is unknown. Has "BCP 6" crossed out in the run-off.

CB 176 NEW YORK PUBLIC LIBRARY: Whei Ling Ty Luu / Boozy Queen (B&C)
Label: BC2 Rel: 25th Feb[8]/17 Mar 1972[3]
Promotional copies with 4-prong centres exist.

CB 177 FICKLE PICKLE: American Pie / Blown Away (B&C)
Label: BC2 Rel: 21 Jan 1972[3]

CB 178 FICKLE PICKLE: California Calling / Doctor Octopus (B&C)
Label: BC2 Rel: 3 Mar 1972[3]

CB 179 RARE BIRD: Sympathy / Devil's High Concern / What You Want To Know / Hammerhead
Label: CH2 Rel: 28 Apr 1972[3]
Solid centre copies with picture sleeve confirmed. Whether 4-prong copies were also issued with picture sleeve is unknown.

CB 180 MARTYN KAYE: Changes / Bad Bad Jo-Jo (B&C)
Label: BC2 Rel: 21 Apr 1972[3/8]

CB 181 GENESIS: Happy The Man / Seven Stones
Label: CH2 Rel: 12 May 1972[3]
Promotional copies with "DJ sample, not for resale" text on the label and stock copies have 4-prong centres. If you bought this on the day of release, then you didn't get a picture sleeve. If you left it a couple of weeks, then you got the picture sleeve. Not fair, eh?

CB 182 COMBINED SUPPORTERS CLUB: We Are The Champions, Part 1 / We Are The Champions, Part 2 (Sing-Along Version) (B&C)
Label: BC2 Rel: 21 Apr 1972[3]

CB 183 SPREADEAGLE: Scipio / ? (NOT RELEASED)
CB 183 SPREADEAGLE: How Can We Be Lost / Nightmare

Label: CH2 Rel: 26 May[3]/9 Jun 1972[8]
Promotional copies with 4-prong centre confirmed and normal picture sleeve copies with solid label confirmed. A different release might have been planned for this catalogue number – the promotional single, BCP 7, has "CB 183 A – 1U" scratched out in the run-off on the Spreadeagle side.

CB 184 WISHFUL THINKING: Clear White Light / Hiroshima (B&C)
Label: BC2 Rel: 5 May 1972[3]
Exists with both solid and 4-prong centres.

CB 185 AUDIENCE: Stand By The Door / Thunder And Lightning
Label: CH2 Rel: 30 Jun 1972[3]

The B&C Discography: 1968 to 1975

CB 186 RAY MORGAN: *Let's Go Where The Good Times Go / San Diego (B&C)*
Label: BC2 Rel: 2 Jun 1972[3]

CB 187 A. AND A. NORTH: *Rosemary / Travelling Band (B&C)*
Label: BC2 Rel: 28 Jul 1972[3]

CB 188 THE JOHNNY ARTHEY ORCHESTRA: *Serenade To Summer / Star Shine (B&C)*
Label: BC2 Rel: 16 Jun 1972[3]
Reissue of CB 118, though not in picture sleeve this time around.

CB 189 ARNOLD CORNS: *Hang On To Yourself / Man In The Middle (B&C)*
Label: BC2 Rel: 25 Aug 1972[3]
Reissue of the previous b–side (CB 149) as an a–side. Later reissued on Mooncrest as MOON 25.

CB 190 JAWBONE: *Gotta Go / Automobile Blues (B&C)*
Label: BC2 Rel: 25 Aug 1972[3/8]
From this point onwards the CB catalogue sequence was used exclusively by Charisma.

CB 191 LINDISFARNE: *All Fall Down / We Can Swing Together (Live Version)*
Label: CH2 Rel: 1 Sep 1972[3]
The picture sleeve includes the Mad Hatter logo, although the single is on the Scroll label design.

CB 192 MONTY PYTHON'S FLYING CIRCUS: *Spam Song / The Concert*
Label: CH2 Rel: 15 Sep 1972[3]
Publishing credit is 1971 (original album incorrectly credits 1970). "Flying Circus" was dropped from subsequent releases. This was the last Charisma single release on the pink scroll label and was also issued on the Mad Hatter label. Some later Mad Hatter copies issued in a picture sleeve, which shows a picture from the "Dirty fork" sketch and not the "Spam" sketch.

CB 193 CAPABILITY BROWN: *Wake Up Little Sister / Windfall*
Label: CH3 Rel: 20 Oct 1972[3]

CB 194 JO'BURG HAWK: *Orang Outang / Dark Side Of The Moon*
Label: CH3 Rel: 17 Nov 1972[3]
Later reissued in Feb 1973 as CB 202 to promote the LP, which was issued in January 1973.

CB 195 STRING DRIVEN THING: *Eddie / Hooked On The Road*
Label: CH3 Rel: Nov[8]/1 Dec 1972[3]

CB 196 AUDIENCE: *Raviole / Hard Cruel World*
Label: CH3 Rel: 10 Nov 1972[3]

CB 197 THE GROUP: *Bovver Boys / Piraeus Football Club / An Open Letter To George Best*
Label: CH3 Rel: 10 Nov 1972[3]

CB 198 BROTHER UNIVERSE: *Christmas Carols: Angels Heard On High / O Come All Ye Faithful / Christmas Carols: We Three Kings Of Orient Are*
Label: CH3 Rel: 24 Nov[3]/7 Dec 1973[3]
Two tracks on the a–side.

The B&C Discography: 1968 to 1975

CB 199   **LINDISFARNE: Court In The Act / Don't Ask Me**
Label: CH3   Rel: 17 Nov 1972[3]

CB 200   **MONTY PYTHON WITH NIEL INNES: Eric The Half A Bee / The Yangtze Song**
Label: CH3   Rel: 17 Nov 1972[3]
Neil Innes has his name incorrectly spelled on labels as "Niel".

CB 200   **THE ARNOLD CORNS: Moonage Daydream / Hang On To Yourself / Man In The Middle (PIRATE PRESSING)**
Label: BC2
This is a pirate pressing and is included merely for information.

CB 201   **GRAHAM BELL: Too Many People / Before You Can Be A Man**
Label: CH3   Rel: 16 Nov[8]/17 Nov 1973[3]

CB 202   **JO'BURG HAWK: Orang Outang / Dark Side Of The Moon**
Label: CH3   Rel: 9 Feb 1973[3/7]
4-prong promotional copies and solid-centred stock copies exist.

CB 203   **STRING DRIVEN THING: Circus / My Real Hero**
Label: CH3   Rel: 16 Feb 1973[3/7]

CB 204   **HOWARD WERTH WITH AUDIENCE: You're Not Smiling / Raviole**
Label: CH3   Rel: 23 Feb 1973[3]
A retrospective issue relegating Audience to second billing behind Charisma solo artist, Werth.

CB 205   **CLIFFORD T. WARD: Gaye / Home Thoughts From Abroad**
Label: CH3   Rel: Mar[7]/13 April 1973[3]

CB 206   **JACK THE LAD: One More Dance / Draught Genius(Polka)**
Label: CH3   Rel: 18 May 1973[3/8]
Picture sleeve.

CB 207   **CAPABILITY BROWN: Midnight Cruiser / Silent Sounds**
Label: CH3   Rel: 22 Jun 1973[3/8]

CB 208   **ALAN HULL: Numbers (Travelling Band) / Drinking Song / One Off Pat**
Label: CH3   Rel: 8 Jun 1973[3/8]
Picture sleeve.

CB 209   **GRAHAM BELL: 60 Minute Man / The Whole Town Wants You Hung**
Label: CH3   Rel: 10 Aug 1973[3]

CB 210   **STRING DRIVEN THING: Are You A Rock And Roller / Night Club**
Label: CH3   Rel: Aug[7]/7 Sep 1973[3]

CB 211   **ALAN HULL: Justanothersadsong / Waiting**
Label: CH3   Rel: 7 Sep 1973[3]

CB 212   **CLIFFORD T. WARD: Wherewithal / Thinking Of Something To Do**
Label: CH3   Rel: 7 Sep 1973[3]

The B&C Discography: 1968 to 1975

CB 213 THE CREATION: Making Time / Painter Man
Label: CH3   Rel: 14 Sep 1973[3/8]
The New Singles miscredits artist as "Pickett/Phillips". Reissue of a–sides from 1966 Planet label singles, PLF 116 and PLF 119.

CB 214 VARIOUS: Lay Lady Lay / Earl's Shuffle
Label: CH3   Rel: Oct 1973[7]
Picture sleeve. Not listed in The New Singles.

CB 215 STRING DRIVEN THING: It's A Game / Are You A Rock And Roller
Label: CH3   Rel: 7 Sep 1973[3]
B–side previously issued as an a–side (CB 210) and has CB 210 scratched out in the run–off.

CB 216 DARIEN SPIRIT: Magic Morning Sun / For All The Years
Label: CH3   Rel: 5 Oct 1973[3]
For All The Years was reissued, again as a b–side, on CB 235.

CB 217 CAPABILITY BROWN: Liar / Keep Death Off The Road (Drive On The Pavement)
Label: CH3   Rel: 26 Oct[3]/Nov 1973[7]
Demo copies exist with release date of either 2nd Nov 1973 or 26th Oct 1973. A–side previously issued on the promotional–only BCP 7. One–sided, white label copies also exist with BCP 9 matrix.

CB 218 JACK THE LAD: Why Can't I Be Satisfied / Make Me Happy
Label: CH3   Rel: 2 Nov 1973[3]

CB 219 KENNY ROWE (AND THE VOICES OF CAPABILITY BROWN): Jesus / ANAWIM: The Water Song
Label: CH3   Rel: 23 Nov 1973[3]

CB 220 DOGGEREL BANK: Tiny Seed Of Love / Down On The Farm
Label: CH3   Rel: 23 Nov 1973[3]/11 Jan 1974[3]

CB 221 CLIFFORD T. WARD: Scullery / To An Air Hostess
Label: CH3   Rel: 30 Nov 1973[3]

CB 222 DARIEN SPIRIT: Magic Morning Sun / Hennessy Gun
Label: CH3   Rel: 8 Feb 1974[3]

CB 223 STRING DRIVEN THING: I'll Sing One For You / To See You
Label: CH3   Rel: Feb[7]/8 Mar 1974[3]

CB 224 GENESIS: I Know What I Like (In Your Wardrobe) / Twilight Alehouse
Label: CH3   Rel: 25 Jan 1974[3/8]
4–prong and solid centred copies exist. A–side is an edited version of the track from Selling England by the Pound (CAS 1074); b–side previously issued on a flexidisc given free with Zigzag.

CB 225 HOWARD CHEN: Lucinda (DEMO?)
CB 225 HOWARD WERTH: Lucinda / Jonah
Label: CH3   Rel: 15 Feb 1974[3]
Howard Chen copies confirmed – though hazy memory suggests that this version may have been a demo with the same track on both sides.

The B&C Discography: 1968 to 1975

CB 226   **NATIONAL YOUTH JAZZ ORCHESTRA: Gatecrasher / Where's Yesterday / NYJO**
Label: CH3   Rel: 15 Feb 1974[3]

CB 227   **SIR JOHN BETJEMAN: A Shropshire Lad / The Cockney Amorist**
Label: CH3   Rel: 8 Mar 1974[3]

CB 228   **LINDISFARNE: Taking Care Of Business / North Country Boy**
Label: CH3   Rel: 29 Mar 1974[3]

CB 229   **THE FRIENDS OF ST. FRANCIS: The Man Who Turned On The World / How Is The World Today?**
Label: CH3   Rel: 22 Mar 1974[8]
Not listed in *The New Singles*. Promotional copies exist with the same track both sides.

CB 230   **BO HANSSON: The Black Riders Flight To The Ford / Wandering Song**
Label: CH3   Rel: 31 May 1974[3]
The a–side is really two segued tracks *Black Riders* and *Flight to the Ford*.

CB 231   **UNICORN: Ooh Mother / Bogtrotter**
Label: CH3   Rel: 21 June 1974[3]

CB 232   **LINDISFARNE: Fog On The Tyne / Mandolin King**
Label: CH3   Rel: 12 July 1974[3]
Fans were not particularly enamoured with *Roll on Ruby*, the new LP, so it was given a push by releasing this old chestnut on single for the first time.

CB 233   **CLIFFORD T. WARD: Jayne (From Andromeda Spiral) / Maybe I'm Right**
Label: CH3   Rel: 23 Aug 1974[3]
Labels state that tracks are from the forthcoming LP, *Escalator* and give the LP catalogue number as CAS 1093. *Escalator*, when released, was CAS 1098 and neither track was included. *Jayne (from Andromeda Spiral)* later appeared on the Philips LP, *No More Rock 'n' Roll* (9109 500), in 1975.

CB 234   **GARY SHEARSTON: I Get A Kick Out Of You / Witnessing**
Label: CH3   Rel: 6 Sep 1974[3]
Very few copies exist on the CH3 label design with full B&C credits.

CB 235   **DARIEN SPIRIT: Rock Your Soul / For All The Years**
Label: CH3   Rel: 4 Oct 1974[3]

CB 236   **G. T. MOORE AND THE REGGAE GUITARS: I'm Still Waiting / Judgement Day**
Label: CH4   Rel: 8 Nov 1974[3]
Promotional issue on CH3 label design, though normal stock copies on CH4 design.

CB 237   **GREEP: Gemini / Tradition**
Label: CH4   Rel: 8 Nov[3]/Oct 1974[7]
Promotional copies with normal b–side confirmed.

CB 238   **GENESIS: Counting Out Time / Riding The Scree**
Label: CH4   Rel: 8 Nov 1974[3]

The B&C Discography: 1968 to 1975

CB 239 **STRING DRIVEN THING: Mrs. O'Reilly / Keep On Moving**
Label: CH4   Rel: 15 Nov 1974[3]
Promotional issue on CH3 label design, though normal stock copies on CH4 design.

CB 240 **BERT JANSCH: In The Bleak Midwinter / One For Jo**
Label: CH4   Rel: 22 Nov 1974[3]

CB 241 **GARY SHEARSTON: Without A Song / Aborigine**
Label: CH4   Rel: 29 Nov 1974[3]

CB 242 **JACK THE LAD: Home Sweet Home / Big Ocean Liner**
Label: CH4   Rel: 3 Jan 1975[3]

CB 243 **NO RELEASE**

CB 244 **CHRIS AND PAULINE ADAMS: If Only The Good Die Young / The City At Night**
Label: CH4   Rel: 24 Jan 1975[3]

CB 245 **RIKKI NADIR: Birthday Special / Shingle Song**
Label: CH4   Rel: 24 Jan 1975[3]
Rikki Nadir was Peter Hammill's punk alter-ego – a full year before the first 'official' UK punk record.

CB 246 **PIERRE COUR: Letter To A Teenage Bride / Love Letter**
Label: CH4   Rel: 14 Feb 1975[3]
A-side sub-credits "(with Orchestra directed by Zack Laurence)". B-side sub-credits "(with Zack Laurence, piano)". Promotional copies have the normal b-side. The female staff at Charisma felt that this single was sexist in the extreme (perhaps Valentine's Day was not the best day for issue) and so there was marked lack of enthusiasm about promoting it. The pressing run was bunged into a cupboard and forgotten about, which might explain why no stock copies have come to light.

CB 247 **STRING DRIVEN THING: Overdrive / Timpani For The Devil**
Label: CH4   Rel: 21 Feb 1975[3]
Promotional copies have the normal b-side. No date of issue stated on press release.

CB 248 **CLIFFORD T. WARD: Jig Saw Girl / Cellophane**
Label: CH4   Rel: 7 Mar 1975[3]
Promotional copies have the normal b-side.

CB 249 **GARY SHEARSTON: Dingo / Back Of Beyond**
Label: CH4   Rel: 14 Mar 1975[3]

CB 250 **GRAHAM BELL: You Need A 60 Minute Man / That's The Way It Is**
Label: CH4   Rel: April 1975[7]
Not listed in *The New Singles*. Promotional copies have the normal b-side. Copy viewed with hand-written date bought of "27th March 1975".

CB 251 **GENESIS: The Carpet Crawlers / The Waiting Room (Evil Jam)**
Label: CH4   Rel: 18 April 1975[3]
A-side is a slightly-edited version of the album track *Carpet Crawl*, B-side is a live version and includes the additional credit "Recorded live at The Shrine, Los Angeles".

CB 252 **DOGGEREL BANK: Mr. Skillicorn Dances / Shopping Around**
Label: see below   Rel: see below
Not listed in *The New Singles*. There is a question mark as to whether this was issued.

CB 253   **JACK THE LAD:** *Gentleman Soldier / Oakey Strike Evictions*
Label: CH4   Rel: 2 May 1975[3]

CB 254   **SIR JOHN BETJEMAN:** *Licorice Fields Of Pontefract / In The Public Gardens*
Label: CH4   Rel: 2 May 1975[3]
Promotional copies have the normal b-side. Any record that includes the line "The strongest legs in Pontefract" is a must for any collection.

CB 255   **UNICORN:** *I'll Believe In You (The Hymn) / Take It Easy*
Label: CH4   Rel: 16 May 1975[3]

Promotional 7" singles (B&C and Charisma)

The BCP sequence has many numbers still unaccounted for. Some may not have been used, or may have been used for just a handful of test pressings. Added to this is the fact that B&C used the sequence across various labels – see the relevant sections in the Action, Pegasus/Peg and People discographies for BCP records on those labels – so it is possible that missing numbers might have been used with other B&C-related labels, such as Trojan. It may take years for information about missing numbers to appear, if it ever does.

CB sequence DJ copy with track discrepancy

CB 141   **AUDIENCE:** *Indian Summer / It Brings A Tear (DJ COPY)*
The two track DJ version includes a 19 February 1970 release date and matrix numbers ("CB. 141A/2U"/"CB. 141A/3U") on labels. The single as later released (in March) had both these tracks on the a-side and had a different version of *Priestess* to that included on the LP (CAS 1012) as b-side.

Custom catalogue numbers

JH 1/JH 2   **JACKSON HEIGHTS:** *Doubting Thomas / Insomnia*
Promotional-only single for the Charisma LP, *King Progress* LP (CAS 1018). Labels are marked "Promotional Copy" and "Not For Resale". The a-side has "JH 1" as the catalogue number, whilst b-side has "JH 2".

GS 1/GS 2   **GENESIS:** *Looking For Someone / Visions Of Angels*
Promotional-only single for the Charisma LP, *Trespass* (CAS 1020). The a-side has "GS 1" as the catalogue number, whilst the b-side has "GS 2".

BD 1/BD 2   **EVERY WHICH WAY:** *Go Placidly / The Light*
Promotional-only single for the Charisma LP, *Every Which Way* (CAS 1021). The a-side has "BD 1" as the catalogue number, whilst the b-side has "BD 2". Labels credit "Brian Davison's Every Witch Way", complete with the misspelling of "Which".

HB 1/HB 2   **HANNIBAL:** *Winds Of Change / Winter (B&C)*
Promotional-only single for the B&C LP, *Hannibal* (CAS 1022). A-side has "HB 1" as the catalogue number and b-side has "HB 2".

BCP sequence

BCP 1   **AUDIENCE:** *Your Not Smiling / Eye To Eye*
Wraparound picture sleeve. A-side spelled as above – the normal issue on CB 156 was corrected to read "You're Not Smiling". Catalogue numbers on labels are "BCP.1A" and "BCP.1B".

The B&C Discography: 1968 to 1975

BCP 2   *CAROL GRIMES & THE RED PRICE BAND: I Don't Wanna Discuss It / ROCK & ROLL ALLSTARS: I'm Walking (B&C)*
Both tracks from the B&C LP, *Battle of the Bands Vol. 1* (BCM 103). Catalogue numbers on labels are "BCP 2A" and "BCP 2B".

BCP 6   *VAN DER GRAAF GENERATOR: Theme One / W*
Normal stock copies (CB 175) have "BCP 6" crossed out in the run-off. This does not seem to have been pressed on the promotional catalogue number (or, at least, no copy has yet come to light in collectors' circles). White label test pressings may turn up with only the BCP matrix.

BCP 7   *SPREADEAGLE: Nightingale Lane [plays Scipio, see below] / CAPABILITY BROWN: Liar*
Picture sleeve with what looks like a Terry Gilliam design. The Spreadeagle track is really *Scipio* – a promotional sheet sent out with the record points this out. Labels marked "For Promotion Only – Not For Sale". Issued to promote Spreadeagle's *The Piece of Paper* (CAS 1055) and Capability Brown's *From Scratch* (CAS 1056) LPs. The Spreadeagle side has "CB 183 A–1U" scratched out in the run-off groove (CB 183 was issued instead with Spreadeagle's *How Can We Be Lost* and *Nightmare*).

BCP 9   *CAPABILITY BROWN: Liar*
One–sided copy exists with hand–written white label. This looks to have been pressed up in advance of *Liar* being issued as a single in its own right on CB 217.

BCP 18   *G.T. MOORE AND THE REGGAE GUITARS: Move It On Up / Painted Ladies*
Copy exists with hand–written white label

Flexidiscs

No cat. no.   *GENESIS: Twilight Alehouse*
One–sided flexidisc with no catalogue number or manufacturing details. The record came in a plain, white envelope complete with fold over top. Although a flexi, this was on thicker 'vinyl' than most. Normal vinyl, white label test pressings exist.
    Originally given away with the Charisma–owned *Zigzag* magazine. Pete Frame, *Zigzag's* editor, said (email sent 12 November 2009) that he thought it was issue 27 – there are also claims online for issue number 41, though with no compelling evidence.
    Copies were also included in the programme/souvenir pack sold on the October 1973 tour. The souvenir pack also included an information sheet, Genesis revolver (whatever that was), D.I.Y dice (whatever those were), poster and sticker.
    In 1976 remaining copies were given free to members of the Genesis Information fan club, by which time *Twilight Alehouse* had long since been given a more permanent release as the b–side of *I Know What I Like (In Your Wardrobe)* (CB 224).

No cat. no.   *MONTY PYTHON: Teach Yourself Heath*
Free with the first pressing of *Monty Python's Previous Record* (CAS 1063). The original 8–track issue (Y8CAS 1063) includes the flexidisc track on Programme 4 (presumably the original cassette issue also includes the flexidisc tracks on side 2). According to *Zigzag's* Pete Frame, copies of the flexidisc may also have been given away with *Zigzag* magazine (email, 12 November 2009).

SO 1259   *MONTY PYTHON: D. P. Gumby Presents "Election '74" / The Lumberjack Song (NOT B&C)*
33⅓ rpm, two–sided flexidisc free with the *New Musical Express* in May 1974 to promote *Live at Drury Lane* (CLASS 4). 50,000 copies were pressed in Holland by Sonopresse B. V. Includes some parts that were edited out of the subsequent LP. Neither pressed not marketed by B&C, but it would be mean to exclude it!

Pegasus and Peg

PEG sequence LPs

PEG 1   **ATOMIC ROOSTER: In Hearing Of**
1. Breakthrough
2. Break The Ice
3. Decision/Indecision
4. A Spoonful Of Bromide Helps The Pulse Rate Go Down

1. Black Snake
2. Head In The Sky
3. The Rock
4. The Price

Label: PE1
Rel: pres. Aug '71

Cassette: ZCPEG 1
8-track: Y8PEG 1

Rel: Apr 1972[2]
Rel: Apr 1972[2]

RRP: £2.50[2]
RRP: £2.60[2]

PEG 2   **RICOTTI AND ALBUQUERQUE: First Wind**
1. Ratsa (Don't Know Why)
2. Lo And Behold
3. Go Out And Get It
4. Don't You Believe Me?
5. New York Windy Day

1. Bobo's Party
2. Didn't Wanna Have To Do It
3. Old Ben Houston
4. The Wind Has No Love
5. Give A Damn

Label: PE1
Rel: pres. Aug '71

Trivia: Melanie's surname is miscredited on the sleeve as "Satka", though the label gets it right.

PEG 3   **THREE MAN ARMY: Third Of A Lifetime**
1. Butter Queen
2. Daze
3. Another Day
4. A Third Of A Lifetime
5. Nice One

1. Three Man Army
2. Agent Man
3. See What I Took
4. Midnight
5. Together

Label: PE1
Rel: pres. Aug '71

PEG 4   **BIG SLEEP: Bluebell Wood**
1. Death Of A Hope
2. Odd Song
3. Free Life
4. Aunty James
5. Saint And Sceptic

1. Bluebell Wood
2. Watching Love Grow
3. When The Sun Was Out

Label: PE1
Rel: pres. Aug '71

PEG 5   **ANDY ROBERTS: Nina And The Dream Tree**
1. Keep My Children Warm
2. I've Seen The Movie
3. 25 Hours A Day/Breakdown/ Welcome Home

1. Good Time Charlie
2. Dream Tree Sequence

Label: PE1
Rel: Oct 1971[1]
RRP: £2.19½[1]

Cassette: ZCPEG 5
8-track: Y8PEG 5

Rel: Jul 1972[2]
Rel: Jul 1972[2]

RRP: £2.25[2]
RRP: £2.35[2]

Sleeve (though not label) includes subcredits "Aslaug's Song" and "Nina's Song" for track 2, side 2.

PEG 6   **MARTIN CARTHY AND DAVE SWARBRICK: Selections**
1. The Man of Burnham Town
2. Creeping Jane
3. The Irish Waterwoman/The Ash Plant
4. Lucy Wan
5. Matt Hyland
6. The Wife Of The Soldier

1. The Banks
2. The Bloody Gardener
3. Grey Daylight/Jenny's Chickens
4. Gentleman Soldier
5. Long Lankin
6. Davy Lowston

Label: PE1
Rel: Oct 1971[1]
RRP: £2.19½[1]

The B&C Discography: 1968 to 1975

Cassette: ZCPEG 6   **Rel:** Jul 1972[2]   **RRP:** £2.25[2]
8–track: Y8PEG 6   **Rel:** Jul 1972[2]   **RRP:** £2.35[2]
"CAS 1046" crossed out in the run–off.

PEG 7   SHIRLEY COLLINS AND THE ALBION COUNTRY BAND: No Roses
1. Claudy Banks
2. The Little Gypsy Girl
3. Banks Of The Bann
4. Murder Of Maria Marten

1. Van Dieman's Land
2. Just As The Tide Was Flowing
3. The White Hare
4. Hal–An–Tow
5. Poor Murdered Woman

Label: PE1
Rel: Oct 1971[1]
RRP: £2.19½[1]

Cassette: ZCPEG 7   **Rel:** Jul 1972[2]   **RRP:** £2.25[2]
8–track: Y8PEG 7   **Rel:** Jul 1972[2] (del: 1977[5])   **RRP:** £2.35[2]
"CAS 1047" crossed out in the run–off. Confirmed on both Pegasus and Peg labels.

PEG 8   FUCHSIA: Fuchsia
1. Gone With The Mouse
2. A Tiny Book
3. Another Nail

1. Shoes And Ships
2. The Nothing Song
3. Me And My Kite
4. Just Anyone

Label: PE1
Rel: Oct 1971[1]
RRP: £2.19½[1]

PEG 9   STEELEYE SPAN: Ten Man Mop, Or Mr. Reservoir Butler Rides Again
1. Gower Wassail
2. Jigs: Paddy Clancey's Jig/ Willie Clancy's Fancy
3. Four Nights Drunk
4. When I Was On Horseback

1. Marrowbones
2. Captain Coulston
3. Reels: Dowd's Favourite/£10 Float/ The Morning Dew
4. Wee Weaver
5. Skewball

Label: PE1
Rel: Nov 1971[1]
RRP: £2.19½[1]

Cassette: ZCPEG 9   **Rel:** Apr 1972[2]   **RRP:** £2.50[2]
8–track: Y8PEG 9   **Rel:** Apr 1972[2]   **RRP:** £2.60[2]
Embossed sleeve. Inner sleeve and 8–page booklet.

PEG 10   NAZARETH: Nazareth
1. Witchdoctor Woman
2. Dear John
3. Empty Arms, Empty Heart
4. I Had A Dream
5. Red Light Lady

1. Fat Man
2. Country Girl
3. Morning Dew
4. The King Is Dead

Label: PE1
Rel: Nov 1971[1]
RRP: £2.19½[1]

Cassette: ZCPEG 10   **Rel:** Sep 1972[2]   **RRP:** £2.35[2]
8–track: Y8PEG 10   **Rel:** Sep 1972[2]   **RRP:** £2.35[2]
Matt sleeve (later Peg copies in glossy sleeve). Track 5, side 1 subtitled "(parts 1 & 2)" on sleeve but not label. There seems to be a mismatch in release dates between tape and LP versions.

PEG 11   RITCHIE FRANCIS: Songbird
1, Song Bird
2. Dizzy Sycamore
3. I'm Not Alone
4. It Will Last
5. My Music

1. Don't You Ask Me Why
2. There's A Time
3. Yet To Come
4. Friends
5. You're Never Gonna Make It
6. To Follow You

Label: PE2
Rel: Mar 1972[1]
RRP: £2.19[1]

Cassette: ZCPEG 11   **Rel:** Apr 1972[2]   **RRP:** £2.50[2]
8–track: Y8PEG 11   **Rel:** Apr 1972[2]   **RRP:** £2.60[2]
The "Pegasus" credit on sleeve amended to read "Peg". First Peg label LP, presumably.

The B&C Discography: 1968 to 1975

PEG 12   MARTIN CARTHY: Shearwater
1. I Was A Young Man
2. Banks Of Green Willow
3. Handsome Polly-O
4. Outlandish Knight
5. He Called For A Candle

1. John Blunt
2. Lord Randall
3. William Taylor
4. Famous Flower Of Serving Men
5. Betsy Bell And Mary Gray

Label: PE2
Rel: Mar 1972[1]
RRP: £2.19[1]

Cassette: ZCPEG 12
8-track: Y8PEG 12
Insert.

Rel: Apr 1972[2]
Rel: Apr 1972[2] (del: 1977[5])

RRP: £2.50[2]
RRP: £2.60[2]

PEG 13   SPIROGYRA: Old Boot Wine
1. Dangerous Dave
2. Van Allen's Belt
3. Runaway
4. Grandad
5. Wings of Thunder

1. World's Eyes
2. Don't Let It Get You
3. Disraeli's Problem
4. A Canterbury Tale

Label: PE2
Rel: Jun 1972[1]
RRP: £2.08[1]

Cassette: ZCPEG 13
8-track: Y8PEG 13

Rel: Jun 1972[2]
Rel: Jun 1972[2]

RRP: £2.25[2]
RRP: £2.35[2]

PEG 14   NAZARETH: Exercises
1. I Will Not Be Led
2. Cat's Eye, Apple Pie
3. In My Time
4. Woke Up This Morning
5. Called Her Name

1. Fool About You
2. Love Now Your Gone
3. Madelaine
4. Sad Song
5. 1692 (Glen Coe Massacre)

Label: PE2
Rel: Jun 1972[1]
RRP: £2.08[1]

Cassette: ZCPEG 14
8-track: Y8PEG 14

Rel: Aug 1972[2]
Rel: Aug 1972[2]

RRP: £2.25[2]
RRP: £2.35[2]

Track listing from labels. Sleeve credits track 2, side 2 as "Love, Now You're Gone".

PS sequence LPs

PS 1   VARIOUS: Clogs
1. Captain Coulston (Steeleye Span)
2. Richmond (Andy Roberts)
3. The Irish Waterwoman/The Ash Plant (Martin Carthy And Dave Swarbrick)
4. The King (Steeleye Span)
5. Poem (Keith Christmas)
6. Murder Of Maria Maren (Shirley Collins)

1. Rave On (Steeleye Span)
2. I Live Not Where I Love (Tim Hart And Maddy Prior)
3. Captain's Log (Spirogira)
4. Rod's Song (Shelagh McDonald)
5. Lord Randall (Martin Carthy)
6. Yarrow (Marc Ellington)
7. Welcome Home (Andy Roberts)

Label: PE2
Rel: Apr 1972[1]
RRP: 99p[1]

Cassette: ZCPS 1
8-track: Y8PS 1

Rel: Jul 1972[2]
Rel: Jul 1972[2]

RRP: £1.35[2]
RRP: £1.59[2]

Subtitled "Folk Sampler". Insert. "99p" price sticker on sleeve. *Richmond* otherwise unavailable.

PS 2   VARIOUS: Club Folk Volume 1
1. The Sailor (Robin Scott)
2. Red And Green Christmas (Nadia Cattouse)
3. Blue Railway Fields (P C Kent)
4. The Barley Straw (Martin Carthy And Dave Swarbrick)
5. Autumn to May (Andy Roberts)
6. Travelling Down (Keith Christmas)

1. Rolling And Tumbling (Synanthesia)
2. Sweet Sunlight (Shelagh McDonald)
3. Our Captain Cried All Hands (Martin Carthy And Dave Swarbrick)
4. Come Join My Orchestra (Al Jones)
5. Disbelief Blues (Mike Hart)
6. Jello (Andy Roberts)

Label: PE2
Rel: Jul 1972[1]
RRP: 99p[1]

The B&C Discography: 1968 to 1975

Textured sleeve. July edition of *The New Albums* credits PS 2 and PS 3 as "This Is Folk Vol 1" and "This Is Folk Vol 2", both with incorrect price of £2.08. August edition lists correct titles and correct price of 99p.

PS 3   VARIOUS: *Club Folk Volume 2*   Label: PE2   Rel: Jul 1972[1]   RRP: 99p[1]

1. Rainy Night Blues (Shelagh McDonald)
2. What I Was Thinking (Al Jones)
3. Trafalgar Square (Synanthesia)
4. Broadened (P. C. Kent)
5. The Sound Of Rain (Robin Scott)
6. B.C. People (Nadia Cattouse)

1. Domeama (Martin Carthy)
2. Where the Soul Of Man Never Dies (Andy Roberts)
3. All Around My Grandmother's Floor (Nadia Cattouse)
4. Bed–Sit Two Step (Keith Christmas)
5. Yawny Morning Song (Mike Hart)
6. Ire And Spottiswoad (Al Jones)

Textured sleeve. Miscredited in the July edition of *The New Albums* – see PS 2 above.

Tape versions of CAS sequence LPs

By the time that B&C released tape versions of LPs on the CAS sequence, the B&C label had been superseded by Pegasus, followed by Peg. Therefore, tape issues were rebranded as Peg issues, though they otherwise kept their CAS sequence numbering (e.g. CAS 1029 became ZCPEG 1029 on cassette and Y8PEG 1029 on 8–track).

ZCPEG 1029 / Y8PEG 1029   STEELEYE SPAN: *Please To See The King*
Rel: Jul 1972[2] (both formats)   RRP: £2.25[2] (cassette)/£2.35[2] (8–track)

ZCPEG 1035 / Y8PEG 1035   TIM HART AND MADDY PRIOR: *Summer Solstice*
Rel: Jul 1972[2] (both formats)   RRP: £2.25[2] (cassette)/£2.35[2] (8–track)

ZCPEG 1045 / Y8PEG 1045   HAROLD McNAIR: *Harold McNair*
Rel: May 1972[2] (both formats)   RRP: £2.25[2] (cassette)/£2.35[2] (8–track)

PGS sequence 7" singles

PGS 1   THREE MAN ARMY: *What's Your Name? / Travelin'*
Label: PE1   Rel: 5 Nov 1971[3]

PGS 2   NAZARETH: *Dear John / Friends*
PGS 2   NAZARETH: *Dear John / Occasional Failure*
Label: see below   Rel: 28 Jan 1972[3]
The New Singles for 28 Jan 1972 credits the b–side as "Occasional Failure", though on this release (PE1) the label credited the b–side as "Friends". The later Peg repress (PE2) credited the b–side as "Occasional Failure". It ought to be pointed out that *Occasional Failure* and *Friends* are the same track. It looks as though the original b–side label was a mistake.

PGS 3   SPIROGYRA: *Dangerous Dave / Captain's Log*
Label: PE2   Rel: 28 Apr 1972[3]
Picture sleeve. A–side is an edited version of the LP track from *Old Boot Wine* (PEG 13).

PGS 4   NAZARETH: *Morning Dew / Spinning Top*
Label: PE2   Rel: 7 Jul 1972[3]

PGS 5   NAZARETH: *If You See My Baby / Hard Living*
Label: PE2   Rel: 15 Sep 1972[3]

PGS 6   **STEELEYE SPAN: Jigs And Reels / Jigs And Reels**
Label: PE2   Rel: 29 Sep 1972[3]
A-side subcredit: "Reels: Dowd's Favourite; £10 Float; The Morning Dew" under the title; b-side subcredit: "Jigs: Bryan O'Lynn; The Hag With The Money; Paddy Clancey's Jig; Willie Clancy's Fancy".

Promotional 7" records

The flexidisc was pressed up to promote the first four LPs, though it is unknown as to where the record was distributed. The BCP sequence was used for promotional singles on several B&C labels. See the B&C/Charisma, Action and People sections for more information on records in the sequence issued on those labels.

Custom catalogue number

SFI M-G1   **VARIOUS: untitled**
1. The Rock (Atomic Rooster)   1. Butter Queen (Three Man Army)
2. New York Windy Day (Ricotti   2. Saint And Sceptic (Big Sleep)
     And Albuquerque)

'Thick' flexidisc. No catalogue number, but the matrix number is "SFI M-G1", which presumably indicates a Sound for Industry pressing. The LP label design is used on both sides, though with no artist nor track credits. A very un-rock 'n' roll spoken word introduction before each track. All tracks edited versions.

BCP sequence

BCP 3   **NAZARETH: Dear John / Witchdoctor Woman / Morning Dew**
Stamped white label and promotional insert. Two tracks on a-side.

BCP 8   **NAZARETH: Fool About You / Woke Up This Morning /**
                Morning Dew
Copies exist with hand-written white labels. Two tracks on a-side.

Mooncrest

From the start, Mooncrest seemed suspiciously similar to the old B&C label. Much like the old B&C label, Mooncrest suffered from an identity crisis with releases evincing a mix of styles from commercial reggae to hard rock, taking in folk and out–and–out pop along the way. Mooncrest also acquired a subsidiary label, Dragon, from Island in August 1973. What with Dragon showcasing Jamaican music from Byron Lee productions, why the label was licensed to Mooncrest and not to Trojan remains a mystery, though perhaps Mooncrest's account books looked rather more healthy than Trojan's at this point?

Long a mystery, though one now solved, is why Mooncrest didn't release cassette or 8–track versions of high–selling Steeleye Span and Nazareth LP reissues. The reason is that B&C still held large stocks of the original Pegasus and Peg tape versions. See the Pegasus and Peg listings for release information and known deletion dates for tape versions.

At least three releases were lost during B&C's liquidation – these were Decameron's *Beyond the Days* LP (despite adverts showing the sleeve appearing in the music press) an EP by their surf/doo–wop alter–egos, The Magnificent Mercury Brothers, and a single by The Fortunes. The listings are not concerned with later Mooncrest releases following the label's resurrection as part of the reconstituted B&C Recordings Ltd.

CREST sequence LPs

Many Mooncrest LPs previously released on B&C or Pegasus/Peg came complete in original sleeves with original labels and inserts until stocks on hand ran out. Sleeves included Mooncrest stickers over the old catalogue numbers. There are plenty of hybrids out there: a) original pre–Mooncrest LP with inserts and Mooncrest sticker over old catalogue number; b) Mooncrest LP with original inserts in original pre–Mooncrest sleeve with Mooncrest sticker over old catalogue number; c) Mooncrest LP in Mooncrest sleeve with original pre–Mooncrest inserts; d) Full Mooncrest issues with no inserts.

LPs up to (probably) CREST 21 were pressed by EMI, but from that point new LPs and further pressings of back catalogue were pressed by Lyntone, and possibly others.

Many sources are confused about original release dates because LPs reissued by the resurrected Mooncrest were given amended credits including a 1976 publication date. Subsequent repressings retained this 1976 publication credit. Original releases are easy to spot because they have the original 37 Soho Square address for B&C Records, whilst the 1976 reissues have Saga's Kensal Road address.

CREST 1   **NAZARETH: Razamanaz**

1. Razamanaz
2. Alcatraz
3. Vigilante Man
4. Woke Up This Morning

1. Night Woman
2. Bad, Bad Boy
3. Sold My Soul
4. Too Bad, Too Bad
5. Broken Down Angel

Rel: Apr 1973[1]
RRP: £2.10[1]/
£2.14[4]

Cassette: ZCRES 1
8–track: Y8RES 1
Original copies include a Mooncrest inner sleeve advertising the first two LPs.

Rel: Jul 1973[2]
Rel: Jul 1973[2]

RRP: £2.35[2]
RRP: £2.35[2]

The B&C Discography: 1968 to 1975

CREST 2   LIGHTHOUSE: Sunny Days
1. Silver Bird
2. Sunny Days
3. You Girl
4. Beneath My Woman
5. Merlin

1. Broken Guitar Blues
2. Letter Home
3. You Give To Me
4. Lonely Places

Rel: Apr 1973[1]
RRP: £2.10[1]/
    £2.14[4]

Cassette: ZCRES 2
8–track: Y8RES 2

Rel: Sep 1973[2]
Rel: Sep 1973[2]

RRP: £2.35[2]
RRP: £2.35[2]

Presumably included advertising inner. Relisted in the July 1973 edition of *The New Records* with a very inaccurate RRP of £1.49.

CREST 3   HOTSHOTS: Snoopy V.s The Red Baron
1. Snoopy V.s The Red Baron
2. Chatanooga Choo Choo
3. Knockin' On The Door
4. Cousin Of Mine
5. You Don't Know Like I know
6. Itsy Bitsy Teeny Weeny Yellow Polka Dot Bikini

1. Battle Of New Orleans
2. What Do You Say
3. Simple Simon Says
4. Yesterday Man
5. Roll Muddy River
6. I Hear You Knockin'

Rel: Oct 1973[1]
RRP: £2.14[1]
Del: 1975[5]

Cassette: ZCRES 3
8–track: Y8RES 3

Rel: Oct 1973[2]
Rel: Oct 1973[2]

RRP: £2.35[2]
RRP: £2.35[2]

Title as above as taken from labels and spine. The sleeve credits "Snoopy V.s Red Baron".

CREST 4   NAZARETH: Loud 'N' Proud
1. Go Down Fighting
2. Not Fakin' It
3. Turn On Your Receiver
4. Teenage Nervous Breakdown
5. Freewheeler

1. This Flight Tonight
2. Child In The Sun
3. The Ballad Of Hollis Brown

Rel: Nov 1973[1]
RRP: £2.14[1]

Cassette: ZCRES 4
8–track: Y8RES 4

Rel: Jan 1974[10]
Rel: Jan 1974[10]

RRP: prob. £2.45
RRP: prob. £2.45

CREST 5   DANDY LIVINGSTONE: Conscious
1. Black Connection
2. Let Me Tell You What's Goin' On
3. Black Star
4. Caribbean Rock
5. Glory Be Ay, Glory Be You

1. Everyday Gets A Little Bit Sweeter
2. I'm a Believer
3. Love Is About to Get Me
4. Jack, the King of the Tramps
5. Check Out Yourself

Rel: Dec 1973[1]
RRP: £2.14[4]/
    £2.25[1]

Cassette: ZCRES 5
8–track: Y8RES 5
Textured sleeve.

Rel: Mar 1974[10]
Rel: Mar 1974[10]

RRP: prob. £2.45
RRP: prob. £2.45

CREST 6   STU NUNNERY: Stu Nunnery
1. The Isle Of Debris
2. And That's Fine With Me
3. Sally From Syracuse
4. Madelaine

1. Lady, It's Time to Go
2. Your Rise
3. Diminished Love
4. The Lady In Waiting
5. Roads

Rel: Feb 1974[4]
RRP: £2.25[4]
Del: 1975[5]

Cassette: ZCRES 6
8–track: Y8RES 6

Rel: May 1974[10]
Rel: May 1974[10]

RRP: prob. £2.45
RRP: prob. £2.45

Track 1, side 2 does not include the comma on the sleeve credits.

The B&C Discography: 1968 to 1975

CREST 7 **BUDDY RICH: The Roar Of '74**
1. Nuttville
2. Kilimanjaro Cookout
3. Big Mac
4. Backwoods Sideman

1. Time Check
2. Prelude To A Kiss
3. Waltz Of The Mushroom Hunters
4. Senator Sam

Rel: Apr 1974[4]
RRP: £2.25[4]
Del: 1975[5]

Cassette: ZCRES 7
8-track: Y8RES 7

Rel: May 1974[2]
Rel: May 1974[2]

RRP: £2.45[2]
RRP: £2.45[2]

CREST 8 **STEELEYE SPAN: Please To See The King**
Rel: Apr[4]/May 1974[1] RRP: £2.25[1] Del: 1976[5]
Refer to CAS 1029 for track listing. B&C copies in hessian feel sleeve were issued with Mooncrest sticker covering the B&C catalogue number and early Mooncrest copies still included the original B&C insert. Original Peg tape releases were still available.

CREST 9 **STEELEYE SPAN: Ten Man Mop, Or Mr. Reservoir Butler Rides Again**
Rel: Apr[4]/May 1974[1] RRP: £2.25[1] Del: 1975[5]
Refer to PEG 9 for track listing. Early Mooncrest reissues came complete in gatefold sleeve and with an 8-page booklet. Later Mooncrest pressings housed in single sleeve without booklet. Original Peg tape releases were still available.

CREST 10 **NAZARETH: Nazareth**
Rel: Apr[4]/Jun 1974[1] RRP: £2.25[1]
Refer to PEG 10 for track listing. Original Peg tape releases were still available.

CREST 11 **SHIRLEY COLLINS AND THE ALBION COUNTRY BAND: No Roses**
Rel: Apr[4]/Jun 1974[1] RRP: £2.25[1]
Refer to PEG 7 for track listing. Early reissues came in the original Pegasus gatefold sleeve with Mooncrest sticker covering the PEG catalogue number. Original Peg tape releases were still available.

CREST 12 **TIM HART AND MADDY PRIOR: Summer Solstice**
Rel: Apr[4]/May 1974[1] RRP: £2.25[1]
Refer to CAS 1035 for track listing. Reissued in original gatefold sleeve design with updated label credits. Original Peg tape releases were still available.

CREST 13 **NO RELEASE**

CREST 14 **NAZARETH: Exercises**
Rel: Apr 1974[4] RRP: £2.25[4]
Refer to PEG 14 for track listing. Reissue still housed in gatefold sleeve. Original Peg tape releases were still available.

CREST 15 **NAZARETH: Rampant**
1. Silver Dollar Forger (Parts 1 & 2)
2. Glad When You're Gone
3. Loved and Lost
4. Shanghai'd in Shanghai

1. Jet Jag
2. Light My Way
3. Sunshine
4. (a) Shapes of Things (b) Space Safari

Rel: Apr[4]/May '74[1]
RRP: £2.25[1]

Cassette: ZCRES 15
8-track: Y8RES 15

Rel: May 1974[2]
Rel: May 1974[2]

RRP: £2.45[2]
RRP: £2.45[2]

Embossed sleeve. Inner sleeve, and dollar sticker insert, many of which got stuck to the rear of the sleeve because the track listing was on the sticker but not on the sleeve rear. Insert credits track 1, side 2 as "Jet Lag" (which sounds rather more likely than the title as included on the label, above). Sticker also shows track 4, side 2 as two tracks, credited as "(4a)" and "(4b)".

The B&C Discography (1968 to 1975)

CREST 16   TIM MOORE: Tim Moore
1. A Fool Like You
2. Second Avenue
3. Charmer
4. Sister Lilac
5. High Feeling

1. I Can Almost See The Light
2. Love Enough
3. Aviation Man
4. When You Close Your Eyes
5. I'll Be Your Time

Rel: May[1]/Jul '74[1]
RRP: £2.25[1]

Cassette: ZCRES 16
8–track: Y8RES 16

Rel: Jun 1974 [2]
Rel: Jun 1974 [2]

RRP: £2.45[2]
RRP: £2.45[2]

CREST 17   VARIOUS: Rave On
1. Rave On (Steeleye Span)
2. The Ploughboy And The Cockney (Tim Hart And Maddy Prior)
3. Western Wynde (Tim Hart And Maddy Prior)
4. Banks Of The Bann (Shirley Collins)
5. Cold Haily Windy Night (Steeleye Span)
6. Let No Man Steal Your Thyme (Shelagh McDonald)
7. Lovely On The Water (Steeleye Span)

1. Just As The Tide Was Flowing (Shirley Collins)
2. Cannily, Cannily (Tim Hart And Maddy Prior)
3. Matt Hyland (Martin Carthy)
4. Of All The Birds (Tim Hart And Maddy Prior)
5. The Bank (Martin Carthy And Dave Swarbrick)
6. Marrowbones (Steeleye Span)

Rel: Jun 1974[1]
RRP: £2.25[1]
Del: 1975[5]

Shirley Collins' tracks do not credit the Albion Country Band. Original issue has matt sleeve with artist photos on rear cover plus compilation, art direction, design and artwork credits. 1976 and later issues in gloss sleeve without artist photos or the above credits. Later pressing has a plain white spine with credits in different positions (cover illustration wraps around from front to back sleeve on original pressing). Relisted in the July 1974 edition of *The New Records* with RRP of £2.45.

CREST 18   IAN MATTHEWS: Journey's From Gospel Oak
1. Knowing The Game
2. Polly
3. Things You Gave Me
4. Mobile Blue
5. Tribute To Hank Williams

1. Met Her On A Plane
2. Bride 1945
3. Franklin Avenue
4. Do Right Woman
5. Sing Me Back Home

Rel: Aug 1974[1]
RRP: £2.25[4]/ £2.45[1]

Cassette: ZCRES 18
8–track: Y8RES 18

Rel: Sep 1974[2]
Rel: Sep 1974[2]

RRP: £2.40[2]
RRP: £2.40[2]

Journey From Gospel Oak was recorded for Vertigo in November 1972, but was rejected, which led to Sandy Roberton placing Matthews with Mooncrest, which was already re–releasing various of Roberton's B&C, Pegasus and Peg albums.

CREST 19   DECAMERON: Mammoth Special
1. Mammoth Special
2. Rock 'N' Roll Woman
3. Just Enough Like Home
4. A Glimpse Of Me
5. Late On Lady Day
6. Breakdown Of The Song

1. The Cheetah
2. Jan
3. Stonehouse
4. Parade
5. The Empty Space

Rel: Sep 1974[1]
RRP: £2.25[4]/ £2.41[1]

Cassette: ZCRES 19
8–track: Y8RES 19

Rel: Sep 1974[2]
Rel: Sep 1974[2]

RRP: £2.40[2]
RRP: £2.40[2]

Insert. Recorded for Vertigo but re–recorded and released on Mooncrest. Al Fenn explains: "... what was to be 'Mammoth Special' was first recorded for Vertigo, again produced by Sandy Roberton [who had produced the first LP for Vertigo] – Vertigo didn't like it, so we parted company and went to Mooncrest. There we recorded most of the tracks again – one or two fell by the wayside and were replaced by newer material, thereby losing the track on which our five fathers sang backing vocals."

The B&C Discography: 1968 to 1975

CREST 20   **NO RELEASE**

CREST 21   **CHILLI WILLI AND THE RED HOT PEPPERS: Bongos Over Balham**

1. Choo Choo Ch'Boogie
2. We Get Along
3. Desert Island Woman
4. All In A Dream
5. Fiddle Diddle

1. Breathe A Little
2. Truck Driving Girl
3. Jungle Song
4. Midnight Bus
5. Just Like The Devil
6. 9 – 5 Songwriting Man

Rel: Oct[4]/Nov '74[1]
RRP: £2.45[1]

Cassette: ZCRES 21
8–track: Y8RES 21

Rel: Oct 1974[2]
Rel: Oct 1974[2]

RRP: £2.40[2]
RRP: £2.40[2]

Inner sleeve. If there were a prize for the best sleeve on Mooncrest then this would win!

CREST 22   **STEELEYE SPAN: Hark The Village Wait**

1. A Calling–On Song
2. The Blacksmith
3. Fisherman's Wife
4. Blackleg Miner
5. Dark–Eyed Sailor
6. Copshawholme Fair

1. All Things Are Quite Silent
2. The Hills Of Glenmore
3. My Johnny Was A Shoemaker
4. Lowlands of Holland
5. Twa Corbies
6. One Night As I Lay On My Bed

Rel: Sep[4]/Nov '74[1]
RRP: £2.25[4]/
£2.45[1]

Cassette: ZCRES 22
8–track: Y8RES 22

Rel: Sep 1974[2]
Rel: Sep 1974[2]

RRP: £2.40[2]
RRP: £2.40[2]

The record was pressed by Lyntone with "LYN 13885" and "LYN 13886" scratched in the run-offs. Original 1970 RCA release (SF 8113) deleted the same month the Mooncrest version was issued [4].

CREST 23   **TIM HART AND MADDY PRIOR: Folk Songs Of Olde England Volume I**

1. Lish Young Buy–a–Broom
2. Adieu Sweet Lovely Nancy
3. Maid That's Deep In Love
4. The Rambling Sailor
5. Bruton Town
6. Farewell Nancy

1. The Daleman's Litany
2. The Brisk Young Butcher
3. The Stately Southerner
4. Who's The Fool Now
5. A Wager A Wager
6. Babes In The Wood
7. Adam And Eve

Rel: Nov 1974[1]
RRP: £2.45[1]

Cassette: ZCRES 23
8–track: Y8RES 23

Rel: Feb 1975[2]
Rel: Feb 1975[2]

RRP: £2.65[2]
RRP: £2.65[2]

Pressed by Lyntone with "LYN 13887" and "LYN 13888" scratched in run-offs (still there on the 1976 issue – probably old stock in new sleeves). The first Mooncrest sleeve was of a patchwork design, titled as above. Reissued by the resurrected Mooncrest label in 1976 with different sleeve design and the amended title "Folk Songs Of Old England–Volume I" ("Old" without the "e"). A much later Mooncrest reissue in yet another redesigned sleeve (with butterflies) reverted to "Olde".

Originally released in 1968 on Tepee (TPRM 104) and also released in 1969 on Tepee offshoot, Ad Rhythm (ARPS 3), in different sleeve design and side 1 and side 2 switched over for no readily explained reason. Both issues credited as "Folk Songs Of Old England" ("Old" without the "e") with the subtitle "Vol. 1" on the original Tepee release and "Volume 1" on the Ad Rhythm reissue. The original Tee Pee release seems to have been in mono only, whilst the Ad Rhythm reissue seems to have been stereo only. Ad Rhythm issue was deleted in 1974[4].

The B&C Discography: 1968 to 1975

CREST 24 **ESRA MOHAWK: Essra Mohawk**
1. New Skins For Old
2. Openin' My Love Doors
3. Full Fledged Woman
4. You're Finally Here
5. Summertime
6. Back In The Spirit

1. You Make Me Come To Pieces
2. I Cannot Forget
3. Song To An Unborn Soul
4. If I'm Gonna Go Crazy With Someone
   It Might As Well Be You
5. Magic Pen

Rel: Feb 1975[1]
RRP: £2.45[1]

Inner sleeve. No tape versions notified to *The New Cassettes & Cartridges* nor *Cassettes & Cartidges*.

CREST 25 **MARTIN CARTHY: Shearwater**
Rel: Feb 1975[4]   RRP: pres. £2.25
Refer to PEG 12 for track listing. Original Peg tape releases were still available.

CREST 26 **TIM HART AND MADDY PRIOR: Folk Songs Of Olde England Volume II**
1. My Son John
2. Earl John
3. Paddy Stole The Rope
4. The Gardener
5. The Bay Of Biscay
6. Queen Eleanor's Confession

1. Horn Of The Hunter
2. Copshawholme Fair
3. Oats And Beans
4. Fiddler's Green
5. Capt. Wedderburn's Courtship
6. Turkey Rhubarb
7. The Bold Fisherman

Rel: 1975
RRP: pres. £2.45

Cassette: ZCRES 26   Rel: May 1975[2]   RRP: £2.65[2]
8–track: Y8RES 26   Rel: May 1975[2]   RRP: £2.65[2]

Track 3, side 2 credited on sleeve as "Oats & Beans & Barley Grows" but as "Oats & Beans" on the label; track 5, side 2 credited on sleeve as "Captain" but as above on the label. The first Mooncrest sleeve was of a patchwork design, titled as above. Reissued by the resurrected Mooncrest label in 1976 with different sleeve design and the amended title "Folk Songs Of Old England–Volume II" ("Old" without the "e"). A much later Mooncrest reissue in yet another redesigned sleeve (with butterflies) reverted to "Olde".

Originally released in 1969 on Tepee (TPRM 105) and also released on Tepee offshoot, Ad Rhythm (ARPS 4) in different sleeve design. Both issues credited as "Folk Songs Of Old England" ("Old" without added "e") with the subtitle "Vol. 2" on the original Tepee release and "Volume 2" on the Ad Rhythm reissue. The original Tee Pee release seems to have been in mono only, whilst the Ad Rhythm reissue seems to have been stereo only. The Ad Rhythm issue deleted in 1974[4].

CREST 27 **NAZARETH: Hair Of The Dog**
1. Hair Of The Dog
2. Miss Misery
3. Guilty
4. Changin' Times

1. Beggars Day
2. Rose In The Heather
3. Whisky Drinkin' Woman
4. Please Don't Judas Me

Rel: Apr 1975[1]
RRP:£2.45[1]

Cassette: ZCRES 27   Rel: May 1975[2]   RRP: £2.65[2]
8–track: Y8RES 27   Rel: May 1975[2]   RRP: £2.65[2]
Inner sleeve.

CREST 28 **DECAMERON: Beyond The Days (NOT RELEASED)**
Rel: Jul 1975[1/4] (see below)   RRP: pres. £2.75[1] (see below)
Despite *Music Master* publications from 1976 onward confidently stating a release date of July 1975 this was caught up in B&C's liquidation and issued instead by Transatlantic as *Third Light* in October 1975[4]. Al Fenn explains: "We recorded *Beyond the Days* with Tom Allom as producer for Mooncrest, with all artwork etc. done (dreadful!) but, unfortunately, B&C went down before its release. We then moved to Transatlantic, and it was released under the title of *Third Light*. The ... non existent ... version ... appears in *Record Collector* ... valued at £25!"

MOON sequence 7" singles

Most, but not all, releases were pressed up with the same track on both sides for promotional use. Where different (and known) this is noted. MOON 50 and 51, were notified to the trade for June 1975 release, but were caught up in B&C's liquidation and remained unreleased (unless anyone out there knows any different, that is). When Mooncrest was resurrected in 1976, these two numbers were reused for the first two new releases, which adds to the argument that the originally intended records were not issued.

MOON 1   NAZARETH: Broken Down Angel / Witchdoctor
Rel: 23 Mar 1973[8]
Promotional copies (same track both sides) came in a yellow, printed die–cut single sleeve with details of the first two Mooncrest 7" releases.

MOON 2   LIBIDO: Hold On To Your Fire / Weren't Born A Man
Rel: 23 Mar 1973[8]
Promotional copies presumably came in promotional sleeves as per MOON 1.

MOON 3   LIGHTHOUSE: Sunny Days / Lonely Places
Rel: 20 Apr 1973[3]

MOON 4   A. AND A. NORTH: My Star / I Love You Because
Rel: 20 Apr 1973[3]

MOON 5   HOTSHOTS: Snoopy Versus The Red Baron / What Do You Say
Rel: 4 May 1973[3]

MOON 6   ROCKMORE WILLIAMS: It Was Her / I'm A Man
Rel: 11 May 1973[8]/11 Jan 1974[3]

MOON 7   OCTOPUS: Hey Na Na / Future Feelings
Rel: 16 Jun[3]/Jul 1973[5]

MOON 8   DONNA MARIE NEWMAN: Born Too Late / Everybody's Saying Goodbye
Rel: 15 Jun 1973[3]

MOON 9   NAZARETH: Bad Bad Boy / Hard Living / Spinning Top
Rel: 6 Jul 1973[3]
Picture sleeve.

MOON 10   WOOLLY: Sunshine Souvenirs / Living And Loving You
Rel: 27 Jul 1973[3/8]

MOON 11   STEVE FELDMAN: Waitin' For The Day To Come / Crystal Dawn
Rel: 10 Aug 1973[3]

MOON 12   HOTSHOTS: Battle Of New Orleans / Knockin' On The Door
Rel: 14 Sep 1973[3]

MOON 13   DANDY LIVINGSTONE: Black Star / All Strung Out On You
Rel: 14 Sep[3]/30 Nov 1973[3]
Labels are modified to include Livingstone's face.

The B&C Discography: 1968 to 1975

MOON 14   NAZARETH: *This Flight Tonight / Called Her Name*
Rel: 21 Sep 1973[3]

MOON 15   ROCKMORE WILLIAMS: *Lady Rock / Junkyard Blues*
Rel: 19 Oct 1973[3]

MOON 16   DONNA MARIE NEWMAN: *Daddy / Sing Me Songs*
Rel: 26 Oct 1973[3]

MOON 17   STU NUNNERY: *Sally From Syracuse / Madelaine*
Rel: 2 Nov 1973[3/8]

MOON 18   CINDY MILLER AND THE FRANCIS COOMBE SCHOOL CHOIR:
Dubious Circus Company / Baby, I Need You Now
Rel: 9 Nov 1973[3]

MOON 19   SPIKE O'BRIEN'S CIRCUS: *Poor Little Fred / Soggy Moggy Bogged Down Blues*
Rel: 16 Nov 1973[3]

MOON 20   HOTSHOTS: *Yesterday Man / Jerusalem Rock*
Rel: 23 Nov 1973[3]
Copies exist with the b–side label on both sides.

MOON 21   WOODY: *Saturday Woman / Zoo Baby*
Rel: 14 Dec 1973[3]
The New Singles miscredits the artist as "Smiley" for reasons unknown.

MOON 22   NAZARETH: *Shanghai'd In Shanghai / Love, Now You're Gone*
Rel: 1 Mar 1974[3]

MOON 23   STU NUNNERY: *Madelaine / Sally From Syracuse*
Rel: 11 Apr 1974[3]
Basically a reissue of MOON 17 with the sides reversed.

MOON 24   GORDON JACKSON: *On The Road To Munich / The Boardroom Reel*
Rel: 26 Apr 1974[3/8]
Jim Parker and Hugh Murphy took time out from working on Charisma's John Betjeman albums to do something similar for *Upstairs, Downstairs* actor, Jackson.

MOON 25   ARNOLD CORNS: *Hang On To Yourself / Man In The Middle*
Rel: 17 May 1974 [3/8] (del: 1976[5])
Reissue of the B&C single, CB 189.

MOON 26   TIM MOORE: *When You Close Your Eyes / Aviation Man*
Rel: May[5]/31 Jun 1974[3]

MOON 27   IAN MATTHEWS: *Met Her On A Plane / Knowing The Game*
Rel: 7 Jun 1974[3]

MOON 28   JONNY SUMMA: *Seventeen / Young Girl*
Rel: 7 Jun 1974[3]

The B&C Discography: 1968 to 1975

MOON 29   ALBATROSS: Rock 'N' Roll Boogie Man / Witchi Witchi Lady
Rel: 5 Jul 1974[3]

MOON 30   HOTSHOTS: Caribbean / Together
Rel: 19 Jul 1974[3]

MOON 31   ROCKMORE WILLIAMS: Roll Me Over Again / Junkyard Blues
Rel: 26 Jul 1974[3]
Junkyard Blues was previously issued as the b-side of MOON 15.

MOON 32   TIM MOORE: Charmer / Second Avenue
Rel: Sep[7]/4 Oct 1974[3]

MOON 33   JOHNNIE RICCO: Run Around Sue / Scamp Stamp
Rel: 4 Oct 1974[3]

MOON 34   DECAMERON: Rock And Roll Away / Twinset And Pearls
Rel: 25 Oct 1974[3]

MOON 35   THE ANGELETTES: I Surrender / Goodbye Jon
Rel: 1 Nov 1974[3]

MOON 36   ALBATROSS: Anything I Want To / Bournemouth Rock
Rel: 8 Nov 1974[3]

MOON 37   NAZARETH: Love Hurts / Down
Rel: 8 Nov 1974[3]

MOON 38   NO RELEASE

MOON 39   SCOTT ENGLISH: Brandy / Lead Me Back
Rel: 31 Jan[3]/Feb 1975[7]

MOON 40   CHILLI WILLI AND THE RED HOT PEPPERS: Breathe A Little / Friday Song
Rel: 7 Feb 1975[3] (del: 1977[5])

MOON 41   TIM MOORE: A Fool Like You / Aviation Man
Rel: 21 Feb 1975[3]
Aviation Man was previously issued as the b-side of MOON 26. Promotional copies have the normal track listing.

MOON 42   ALBATROSS: Darlin' / The Band Played On
Rel: 28 Feb 1975[3] (del: 1978[5])

MOON 43   PLAYGROUNDS: This Old Man / Always Friends
Rel: 21 Mar 1975[3]
Promotional copies have normal track listing but with a large "A" printed on the a-side.

MOON 44   NAZARETH: Hair Of The Dog / Too Bad, Too Sad
Rel: 14 Mar 1975[3]

The B&C Discography: 1968 to 1975

MOON 45   **DECAMERON: Breakdown Of The Song / Twinset And Pearls**
Rel: 11 Apr 1975[3] (del: 1977[5])
Twinset and Pearls previously issued as the b–side of MOON 34. Promotional copies have normal track listing.

MOON 46   **ARLAN GREEN: Rock Hotel / Rock Hotel (PROMOS ONLY?)**
Rel: not advised to *The New Singles*
The only copies to come to light are promotional pressings with *Rock Hotel* on both sides. It is just possible that there are stock copies out there, but it is becoming increasingly unlikely

---

MOON 47   **NAZARETH: My White Bicycle / Miss Misery**
Rel: 25 Apr 1975[3]

MOON 48   **NO RELEASE**

MOON 49   **GARY BENSON: Don't Throw It All Away / This House**
Rel: 6 Jun 1975[3]

MOON 50   **MAGNIFICENT MERCURY BROTHERS: New Girl In School / What About Us / Why Do Fools Fall In Love / (I'm Not A) Juvenile Delinquent (NOT RELEASED)**
Rel: 27 Jun 1975[3]
Scheduled for release in late June 1975 but caught up in B&C's liquidation and not issued. The Magnificent Mercury Brothers were really Decameron. Al Fenn explains: "... the Magnificent Mercury Brothers songs were destined for an EP on Mooncrest – the whole thing came from the fact that we would slip a Beach Boys/doo wop song into our normal set (light relief from some of the rest of our songs). These would go down a storm with folk club audiences ... [Mooncrest label manager] Jim Flynn saw this reaction more than once, and said we had to record them. They were recorded at the same time as *Beyond the Days* ... but never got to the artwork stage ... Transatlantic took them on, and cautiously released *New Girl In School* which got onto the Radio One playlist ..."
Transatlantic released the four tracks as two singles, *New Girl In School / What About Us* (BIG 532) and *Why Do Fools Fall In Love / (I'm Not A) Juvenile Delinquent* (BIG 536). *New Girl In School* got a reissue on Transatlantic's new Logo imprint in 1978 (GO 107).
Moon 50 was subsequently used by the resurrected Mooncrest label in 1976 for *Rave On/The King/False Knight On The Road* by Steeleye Span.

MOON 51   **THE FORTUNES: These Are The Good Old Days / Holy Roller (NOT RELEASED)**
Rel: 20 Jun 1975[3] (del: 1977[5])
Although notified as a June 1975 release to trade publications, it is more than likely that this was caught up in the B&C liquidation and that the first distribution (if indeed any were pressed) was by the resurrected Trojan. The single is listed as unreleased on the Fortunes' official fan website (http://www.songwriters.4t.com/) and this would seem to be accurate in that no copies are known to have cropped up on the collectors' circuit (other than rumour of a one–sided Trident acetate, that is). If this latter is true then the notified deletion date seems a little mysterious. Perhaps 1977 represents the date at which the resurrected Trojan noticed that it didn't hold any stock (and not realising that it never had).
Moon 51 was subsequently used by the resurrected Mooncrest label in 1976 for *Jungle Rock/Girl In Red* by Shakin' Stevens and the Sunsets.

People

Various releases, including cassette and 8–track versions, were listed as on catalogue as late as 1979. As from 1976, these were listed as distributed by the resurrected Trojan, and probably represented unsold original stock. The only record confirmed as repressed post-liquidation was Donna Summer's *The Hostage* (PEO 115), this following her recent success on the GTO label. PEO 118 may also have been repressed.

PLEO sequence LPs

PLEO 1 — **REUBEN WILSON: The Cisco Kid**
1. The Cisco Kid
2. The Last Tango In Paris
3. Superfly
4. We've Only Just Begun

1. Snaps
2. Groove Grease
3. The Look Of Love

Rel: Nov 1973[1]
RRP: £1.99[1]/
£2.14[4]
Del: 1975[5]

Cassette: ZCPLE 1
8–track: Y8PLE

Rel: May 1974[2](del 1977[5])
Rel: May 1974[2] (del 1977[5])

RRP: £2.45[2]
RRP: £2.45[2]

PLEO 2 — **LARRY WILLIS: Inner Crisis**
1. Out On The Cost
2. 153rd Street Theme
3. Inner Crisis

1. Bahamian Street Dance
2. For A Friend
3. Journey's End

Rel: Nov 1973[1]
RRP: £1.99[1]/
£2.14[4]
Del: 1975[5]

Cassette: ZCPLE 2
8–track: Y8PLE 2

Rel: May 1974[2]
Rel: May 1974[2] (del 1977[5])

RRP: £2.45[2]
RRP: £2.45[2]

PLEO 3 — **O'DONEL LEVY: Dawn Of A New Day**
1. Dawn Of A New Day
2. Baa Waa
3. I Wanna Be Where You Are
4. Where Is The Love
5. People Make The World Go Round

1. Maiden Voyage
2. Super Woman
3. I Want To Make It With You
4. Goin' On To Detroit

Rel: Nov 1973[1]
RRP: £1.99[1]/
£2.14[4]
Del: 1975[5]

Cassette: ZCPLE 3
8–track: Y8PLE 3

Rel: May 1974[2]
Rel: May 1974[2] (del 1977[5])

RRP: £2.45[2]
RRP: £2.45[2]

PLEO 4 — **JUNIOR PARKER: You Don't Have To Be Black To Love The Blues**
1. Five Years Long
2. Tin Pan Alley
3. Blue Shadows Falling
4. That's Alright
5. Way Back Home

1. I Need Love So Bad
2. Look On Yonders Wall
3. Man Or Mouse
4. Sweet Home Chicago
5. I Like Your Smile

Rel: Nov 1973[1]
RRP: £1.99[1]/
£2.14[4]
Del: 1975[5]

Cassette: ZCPLE 4
8–track: Y8PLE 4

Rel: May 1974[2]
Rel: May 1974[2]

RRP: £2.45[2]
RRP: £2.45[2]

PLEO 5 — **RAMON MORRIS: Sweet Sister Funk**
1. First Come, First Serve
2. Wijinia
3. Sweet Sister Funk

1. Sweat
2. Don't Ask Me
3. Lord Sideways
4. People Make The World Go Round

Rel: Nov 1973[1]
RRP: £1.99[1]/
£2.14[4]
Del: 1975[5]

Cassette: ZCPLE 5
8–track: Y8PLE 5

Rel: May 1974[2]
Rel: May 1974[2] (del 1977[5])

RRP: £2.45[2]
RRP: £2.45[2]

The B&C Discography: 1968 to 1975

PLEO 6   CARMEN McRAE: It Takes A Whole Lot Of Human Feeling
1. It Takes A Whole Lot of Human Feeling
2. I Fall In Love Too Easily
3. Hey John
4. Where Are The Words
5. Nice Work If You Can Get It

1. Straighten Up And Fly Right
2. Inside A Silent Tear
3. Imagination
4. The Right To Love
5. All The Things You Are

Rel: Nov 1973[1]
RRP: £1.99[1]/
£2.14[5]

Cassette: ZCPLE 6
8-track: Y8PLE 6

Rel: May 1974[2] (del 1977[5])
Rel: May 1974[2] (del 1977[5])

RRP: £2.45[2]
RRP: £2.45[2]

PLEO 7   DELLA REESE: Let Me In Your Life
1. Let Me In Your Life
2. Lay Baby Lay
3. If Loving You Is Wrong (I Don't Want To Be Right)
4. Being Green
5. Let's Start All Over Again

1. Fire And Rain/Bye Bye Love
2. Never Can Say Good-Bye/Let's Stay Together
3. Funny
4. Who Is She And What Is She To You

Rel: Nov 1973[1]
RRP: £1.99[1]/
£2.14[4]
Del: 1975[5]

Cassette: ZCPLE 7
8-track: Y8PLE 7

Rel: May 1974[2]
Rel: May 1974[2]

RRP: £2.45[2]
RRP: £2.45[2]

PLEO 8   NO RELEASE

PLEO 9   CHICK COREA: Sundance
1. The Brain
2. Song Of Wind

1. Converge
2. Sundance

Rel: Feb 1974[4]
RRP: £2.25[4]

Cassette: ZCPLE 9
8-track: Y8PLE 9

Rel: Jun 1974[2] (del 1977[5])
Rel: Jun 1974[2]

RRP: £2.45[2]
RRP: £2.45[2]

PLEO 10   GROOVE HOLMES: American Pie
1. American Pie
2. St. Thomas
3. Catherine
4. Fingers

1. It's Impossible
2. Rainy Day
3. Who Can I Turn To

Rel: Feb 1974[4]
RRP: £2.25[4]

Cassette: ZCPLE 10
8-track: Y8PLE 10

Rel: Jul 1974[2]
Rel: Jul 1974[2]

RRP: £2.45[2]
RRP: £2.45[2]

PLEO 11   DAKOTA STATON: Madame Foo-Foo
1. Let It Be Me
2. Congratulations To Someone
3. Let Me Off Uptown
4. A House Is Not A Home
5. Blues For Tasty

1. A Losing Battle
2. Deep In A Dream
3. Confessin' The Blues
4. Candy
5. Moonglow

Rel: Feb[4]/Mar '74[1]
RRP: £2.25[1]

Cassette: ZCPLE 11
8-track: Y8PLE 11

Rel: Jun 1974[2]
Rel: Jun 1974[2] (del 1977[5])

RRP: £2.45[2]
RRP: £2.45[2]

PLEO 12   DORIS TROY: Stretchin' Out
1. Stretchin' Out
2. All I Have Is Written In Your Eyes
3. Don't Let Me Be Lonely Tonight
4. Jesus Is All The World To Me
5. Reconsider Our Love
6. In My Father's Home

1. Black Star
2. Way Back Home
3. Don't Tell Your Mama
4. Tell Me
5. Listen To The Music

Rel: Mar 1974[1]
RRP: £2.25[1]
Del: 1975[5]

The B&C Discography: 1968 to 1975

Cassette: ZCPLE 12	Rel: Jun 1974[2]	RRP: £2.45[2]
8–track: Y8PLE 12	Rel: Jun 1974[2] (del 1977[5])	RRP: £2.45[2]

PLEO 13   BABY WASHINGTON AND DON GARDNER: Lay A Little Lovin' On Me

1. Lay A Little Lovin' On Me
2. Forever
3. I've Got To Break Away (Washington)
4. Just Stand By Me (Gardner)
5. Baby Let Me Get Close To You

1. I Just Want To Be Near To You
2. Is It True I Fell In Love Again
3. Carefree (Washington)
4. We're Gonna Make It Big (Gardner)
5. Can't Get Over Losing You (Washington)

Rel: Mar 1974[1]
RRP: £2.25[1]
Del: 1975[5]

Cassette: ZCPLE 13	Rel: Jul 1974[10]	RRP: prob. £2.45
8–track: Y8PLE 13	Rel: Jul 1974[10] (del 1977[5])	RRP: prob. £2.45

Some tracks are solo, as indicated above, whilst the rest are joint recordings.

PLEO 14   JIMMY McGRIFF: Fly Dude

1. Everyday I Have The Blues
2. Jumping The Blues
3. Healin' Feeling
4. Cotton Boy Blues

1. Yardbird Suite
2. The Groove Fly
3. It's You I Adore
4. Butterfly

Rel: Apr[4]/May '74[1]
RRP: £2.25[1]

Cassette: ZCPLE 14	Rel: Jul 1974[2]	RRP: £2.45[2]
8–track: Y8PLE 14	Rel: Jul 1974[2] (del 1977[5])	RRP: £2.45[2]

PLEO 15   JOE THOMAS: Joy Of Cookin'

1. Joyful, Joyful
2. Down Home
3. Chile Con Carmen

1. Thank You (Fall Etin Me Be Mice Elf Agin)
2. Soul Sermon
3. Mike
4. Dr. Ritota

Rel: Feb[4]/May[1]/Jun 1974[1]
RRP: £2.25[1]

Cassette: ZCPLE 15	Rel: Jul 1974[2]	RRP: £2.45[2]
8–track: Y8PLE 15	Rel: Jul 1974[2] (del 1977[5])	RRP: £2.45[2]

PLEO 16   JIMMY McGRIFF AND GROOVE HOLMES: Giants Of The Organ Come Together

1. Licks A' Plenty
2. Out Of Nowhere
3. The Squirrel

1. Finger Lickin' Good
2. How High The Moon
3. Things Ain't What They Used To Be

Rel: Apr[4]/May '74[1]
RRP: £2.25[1]

Cassette: ZCPLE 16	Rel: Jun 1974[2]	RRP: £2.45[2]
8–track: Y8PLE 16	Rel: Jun 1974[2] (del 1977[5])	RRP: £2.45[2]

8–track deleted 1977 if you look under McGriff, but still on catalogue if you look under Holmes!

PLEO 17   JIMMY McGRIFF: Friday The 13th. Cook County Jail.

1. Freedom Suite, Part I
2. Freedom Suite, Part II

1. Green Dolphin Street
2. Everything Happens To Me
3. Cherokee

Rel: unconfirmed
RRP: prob. £2.25

Cassette: ZCPLE 17	Rel: Jul 1974[2]	RRP: £2.45[2]
8–track: Y8PLE 17	Rel: Jul 1974[2] (del 1977[5])	RRP: £2.45[2]

The B&C Discography: 1968 to 1975

PLEO 18   JUNIOR PARKER: Love Ain't Nothin' But A Business Going On

1. Love Ain't Nothin' But A Business Goin' On
2. The Outside Man
3. Darling Depend On Me
4. Taxman
5. Rivers Invitation

1. I Wonder Where Our Love Has Gone
2. Just To Hold My Hand
3. You Know I Love You
4. Lady Madonna
5. Tomorrow Never Knows

Rel: between Apr and Jun '74[12]
RRP: £2.25[4]
Del: 1975[5]

Cassette: ZCPLE 18
8-track: Y8PLE 18

Rel: Jul 1974[2]
Rel: Jul 1974[2]

RRP: £2.45[2]
RRP: £2.45[2]

PLEO 19   JIMMY McGRIFF: Let's Stay Together

1. Let's Stay Together
2. Tiki
3. The Theme From Shaft
4. What's Going On

1 Old Grad Dad
2. Georgia On My Mind
3. April In Paris

Rel: unconfirmed
RRP: £2.25[4]

Cassette: ZCPLE 19
8-track: Y8PLE 19

Rel: Sep 1974[2]
Rel: Sep 1974[2] (del 1977[5])

RRP: £2.40[2]
RRP: £2.40[2]

PLEO 20   RUEBEN WILSON: The Sweet Life

1. Inner City Blues
2. Creampuff
3. Sugar

1. I'll Take You There
2. The Sweet Life
3. Never Can Say Goodbye

Rel: Jun 1974[4]
RRP: £2.25[4]
Del: 1975[5]

Cassette: ZCPLE 20
8-track: Y8PLE 20

Rel: Sep 1974[2] (del 1977[5])
Rel: Sep 1974[2] (del 1977[5])

RRP: £2.45[2]
RRP: £2.45[2]

PLEO 21   O'DONEL LEVY: Breeding Of Mind

1. We've Only Just Begun
2. It's Too Late
3. Breeding Of Mind
4. Cherries
5. On Broadway

1. Ideal
2. Never Can Say Goodbye
3. Let's Stay Together
4. The Chocolate Horse
5. Angel Eyes

Rel: Jun 1974[4]
RRP: £2.25[4]
Del: 1975[5]

Cassette: ZCPLE 21
8-track: Y8PLE 21

Rel: Sep 1974[2]
Rel: Sep 1974[2] (del 1977[5])

RRP: £2.40[2]
RRP: £2.40[2]

PLEO 22   GEORGE FREEMAN: New Improved Funk

1. New Improved Funk
2. Daffy
3. Happy Fingers
4. All In The Game
5. Big Finish

1. Guitar Lover Man
2. Good Morning Heartache
3. Some Enchanted Evening
4. Confirmed Truth

Rel: Jun 1974[4]
RRP: £2.25[4]

Cassette: ZCPLE 22
8-track: Y8PLE 22

Rel: Sep 1974[2]
Rel: Sep 1974[2] (del: 1977[5])

RRP: £2.40[2]
RRP: £2.40[2]

PLEO 23   JIMMY McGRIFF: If You're Ready Come Go With Me

1. If You're Ready Come Go With Me
2. Shuckin' And Jivin'
3. Dig On It
4. Bug Out
5. Fat Cakes
6. Super Funk

1. Let's Stay Together
2. The Bird
3. Plain Brown Bag
4. Jumpin' The Blues
5. Tiki
6. Ain't It Funky Now

Rel: Jun 1974[4]
RRP: £2.25[4]

No tape versions notified to *The New Cassettes & Cartridges* nor *Cassettes & Cartridges*.

The B&C Discography: 1968 to 1975

PLEO 24   *VARIOUS: Super Sweet Soul*
1. Get On Board (Wee Three)
2. Rockspring Rail Road Station
   (Tom Green)
3. Black Foxy Woman
   (Chuck Armstrong)
4. Care Free (Baby Washington)
5. Check Your Bucket (Eddie Bo)
6. Super Sweet Girl Of Mine
   (Five Miles Out)
7. We're Gonna Make It Big
   (Don Gardner)
8. My Sweet Baby (The Esquires)

1. Get It While You Can
   (Wilbert Harrison)
2. Dynamite Explodes
   (Gentle Persuasion)
3. Get Some (Wee Willie And
   The Winners)
4. It Ain't Easy (Brother James And
   Sugar Mama)
5. Set Your Mind Free (Five Miles Out)
6. Just Keep On Truckin'
   (Backyard Heavies)
7. Soul Makossa (The Gaytones)
8. Funky Buttercup (The Chosen Few)

Rel: Jul[4]/Aug '74[1]
RRP: £2.25[4]/
£2.45[1]

Cassette: ZCPLE 24
8–track: Y8PLE 24

Rel: Sep 1974[2]
Rel: Sep 1974[2] (del 1977[5])

RRP: £2.45[2]
RRP: £2.45[2]

PLEO 25   *THE BROTHERS: Disco–Soul*
1. Get Dancin'
2. Never Can Say Goodbye
3. Thanks A Million
4. In the Pocket
5. Kung Fu Fighting

1. You're The First, The Last, My
   Everything
2. Fire
3. Everybody Loves A Winner
4. Are You Ready For This
5. Doctor's Orders

Rel: Apr 1975[1/4]
RRP: £2.45[1]

No tape versions notified to T*he New Cassettes & Cartridges* not *Cassettes & Cartridges.*

PLED sequence double LP

PLED 501   *JIMMY McGRIFF: Black And Blues*
Record 1, side 1
1. Blue Groove Part 1
2. Blues For A Broken Down Funky
   Old Bus
3. Mocha

Record 1, side 2
1. Harp–er
2. Lonesome Road
3. Mack The Knife

Rel: Nov 1973[1]/
Mar 1974[1]
RRP: £3.49[1]

Record 2, side 1
1. Bahama
2. Amen
3. Hey, Mrs Jones

Record 2, side 2
1. Blue Groove Part 2
2. Penthouse Serenade
3. Pennies From Heaven

Cassette: ZCPLD 501
8–track: Y8PLD 501

Rel: May 1974[1]
Rel: May 1974[1] (del 1977[5])

RRP: £3.20[1]
RRP: £3.20[1]

PLE sequence tape–only release

ZCPLE 101/Y8PLE 101   VARIOUS: Listen To The People

1. Listen To The Music (Doris Troy)
2. Tomorrow Never Knows (Junior Parker)
3. Things Ain't What They Used To Be* (Jimmy McGriff And Groove Holmes)
4. I'll Take You There (Reubin Wilson)
5. Sundance* (Chick Corea)
6. Thank You (Joe Thomas)
7. Dynamite Explodes (Gentle Persuasion)
8. Forever (Baby Washington And Don Gardner)
9. Cherokee (Lucky Thompson)
10. Where Is The Love (O'Donel Levy)
11. Out On The Coast (Larry Willis)
12. Let's Start Over All Again (Della Reese)

1. People Make The World Go Round (Ramon Morris)
2. We're Gonna Make It Big (Don Gardner)
3. I Need Your Love So Bad (Junior Parker)
4. American Pie (Groove Holmes)
5. A House Is Not A Home (Dakota Staton)
6. Never Can Say Goodbye (Reuben Wilson)
7. Lonely Days Lonely Nights (Don Downing)
8. Get On Board (Wee Three)
9. Straighten Up And Fly Right (Carmen McRae)
10. New Improved Funk (George Freeman)
11. Breeding Of Mind (O'Donel Levy)
12. Just Can't Get You Out Of My Mind (Baby Washington)
13. Amen (Jimmy McGriff)

Cassette: ZCPEO 101   Rel: Jul 1974[2]   RRP: £2.45[2]
8–track: Y8PEO 101   Rel: Jul 1974[2] (del 1977[5])   RRP: £2.45[2]
Track listing from the cassette version. The two tracks marked * are edited versions.

PEO sequence 7"singles

As per B&C policy many releases were pressed up with the same track on both sides for promotional use. Where different (and known) this is noted. Some singles were issued in a company sleeve advertising *Black Music* magazine on one side with adverts for People, Ashanti, Dragon and Trojan product on the other.

PEO 101   BABY WASHINGTON AND DON GARDNER: Forever / Baby Let Me Get Close To You
Rel: 20 Jul[8]/27 Jul 1973[3]/Mar 1974[5]
Promotional copies have same track listing as stock copies. *Music Master* (5th ed.) lists release date as both July 1973 and March 1974.

PEO 102   DON DOWNING: Lonely Days, Lonely Nights / I'm So Proud Of You
Rel: 24 Aug 1973[3]

PEO 103   GENTLE PERSUASION: Dynamite Explodes / Bring It On Home
Rel: 19 Oct 1973[3/8]

PEO 104   WEE THREE: Get On Board / Get On Board (Instrumental)
Rel: 26 Oct 1973[3/8]

PEO 105   BABY WASHINGTON: Just Can't Get You Out of My Mind / You (Just A Dream)
Rel: 2 Nov 1973[3]
Promotional copies have same track listing as stock copies.

The B&C Discography: 1968 to 1975

PEO 106   *DELLA REECE: Who Is She And What Is She To You / If Loving You Is Wrong (I Don't Want To Be Right)*
Rel: 11 Jan[3]/1 Mar 1974[3]

PEO 107   *BABY WASHINGTON: I've Got To Break Away / Can't Get Over Losing You*
Rel: 15 Feb 1974[3]

PEO 108   *DON DOWNING: Dream World / The Miracle*
Rel: 8 Mar 1974[3] (del: 1976[5])

PEO 109   *RUEBEN WILSON: I'll Take You There / The Cisco Kid*
Rel: 29 Mar 1974[3]

PEO 110   *KRISSI K: Stick Up / Who Do You Think You Are*
Rel: 10 May 1974[3]

PEO 111   *WESTSIDE: Running In And Out Of My Life / Highway Demon*
Rel: 17 May 1974[3]

PEO 112   *DORIS TROY: Stretchin' Out / Don't Tell Your Mama*
Rel: 31 May 1974[3]

PEO 113   *J. KELLY AND THE PREMIERS: She Calls Me Baby / Signed, Sealed And Delivered*
Rel: not notified to *The New Singles*

PEO 114   *BARRY SMITH: Hold On To It / Hold On to It (Version)*
Rel: not notified to *The New Singles*

PEO 115   *DONNA SUMMER: The Hostage / Let's Work Together Now*
Rel: 4 Oct 1974[3]
Original copies have four prong die-cut centres. Later, solid-centre copies exist with updated label credits – these were issued by the resuscitated Trojan during September 1976[5] to capitalise on Summer's two 1976 chart successes on the GTO label.

PEO 116   *WEE WILLIE AND THE WINNERS: I Don't Know What You Got But I Know What You Need (Vocal) / I Don't Know What You Got But I Know What You Need (Instrumental?)*
Rel: 8 Nov[3]/11 Nov 1974[8]
Various recent sources list "(Part 1)" and "(Part 2)" after the titles. However, the a-side suffix as above is confirmed (on demo copies at least). The b-side suffix is not confirmed. US copies on Shotgun include "Part I" and "Part II".

PEO 117   *JIMMY JAMES AND THE VAGABONDS: Help Yourself / Why*
Rel: not notified to *The New Singles*
This was later issued on Trojan as TOP 1 in May 1975[3/5] and again on the resurrected Trojan label's Miami sub label as MIA 404 in September 1976[5].

PEO 118   *THE BROTHERS: In The Pocket / Everybody Loves A Winner*
Rel: 18 Apr 1975[3] (del: 1977[5])
Some copies include a Trojan logo on the labels. These have differences in sizing and placing of various credits and include a 1975 publication date, whilst the normal version says 1974. The guess is that this was repressed by the resurrected Trojan label.

PEO 119   **BARRY SMITH: Hold On To It / Hold On To It (Version)**
Rel: 13 Jun 1975[3]/Jul 1975[5]
This seems to be a straight reissue of PEO 114.

Promotional 7" EP

The BCP sequence was used over several B&C–related labels. Most so far identified were for B&C, Charisma or Pegasus/Peg artists. Only one record has been discovered with People label material, and that only on one side with the other dedicated to Action label material. All tracks are excerpts.

BCP 16   **VARIOUS: untitled**

1. Forever (Don Gardner And
    Baby Washington)
2. Lonely Days, Lonely Nights
    (Don Downing)

1. Check Your Bucket (Eddie Bo)
2. Get It While You Can
    Wilbert Harrison)

Label: see below

A–side label is the People label design, whilst the b–side is the Action label design (AC3).

Dragon

Island set up Dragon in early 1973 to showcase Byron Lee's productions. In August 1973 Mooncrest acquired the license for marketing, distribution and promotion. All LPs were redistributed by Mooncrest with updated sleeve and label credits except for *The Dynamic Sounds Of Jamaica Vol 1* (HELP 9), which remained on catalogue as an Island release as late as 1979. Other Dragon label records were also listed as on catalogue as late as 1979, these now distributed by Trojan (most probably represented unsold original stock).

DRLS sequence LPs

Island-era releases

DRLS 5001   BYRON LEE AND THE DRAGONAIRES: Reggay Roun' The World

1. Breakfast In Bed
2. Cotton Jenny
3. Three Bells
4. Howdy Tenky
5. Popcorn
6. Smoke Gets In Your Eyes

1. Black On
2. City Of New Orleans
3. In The Mood
4. Your Love Is Amazing
5. Back Stabbers
6. Spanish Lace

Rel: 1973
RRP: £2.14[4]

Cassette: ZCDRL 5001   Rel: Sep 1974[2]   RRP: £2.40[2]
8-track: Y8DRL 5001   Rel: Sep 1974[2] (del 1977[5])   RRP: £2.40[2]

Title above as credited on labels: sleeve credits "Reggae Around The World". Original release via Island. Later copies confirmed with "Marketed by B&C Records" text on labels and sleeve.

DRLS 5002   TOOTS AND THE MAYTELS: Funky Kingston

1. Sit Right Down
2. Pomps And Pride
3. Louie Louie
4. I Can't Believe

1. Redemption Song
2. Daddy
3. Funky Kingston
4. It Was Written Down

Rel: 1973
RRP: £2.14[4]

Track 2, side 1 as credited on label: sleeve credits "Pomp and Pride". Later copies replaced Island credits with "Marketed by B&C Records". Following B&C's liquidation, Island reissued this as ILPS 9186 in April 1976[5] but the resurrected B&C/Trojan also reissued it on the original catalogue number in June 1976. It is possible that this latter reissue was really a redistribution of unsold B&C-era stock. No tape versions notified to *The New Cassettes & Cartridges* nor *Cassettes & Cartridges* though probably released at some point either by Island or Mooncrest, which a 1977 deletion date[5] suggests.

Mooncrest-era releases

DRLS 5003   VARIOUS: 20 Dragon Hits

1. I'm So Fed Up (Rocking Horse)
2. Happy Homecoming (Fabulous Flames)
3. What A Festival (Eric Donaldson)
4. Say Wonderful Things (Ken Parker)
5. Festival Tide (Marvin Brooks)
6. Rasta No Born (Jackie Brown)
7. Watergate Affair (Tommy McCook)
8. Our Rendezvous (Freddie McKay)
9. Stages In Life (Dennis Brown)
10. Dr. Who (I. Roy)

1. Conqueror (Stranger And Gladdy)
2. Version Festival (I. Roy And Eric)
3. I Wonder (Jimmy London)
4. The Great Tommy McCook (Tommy McCook)
5. Hot Cross Bun (Big Youth)
6. Happiness (Kitty)
7. Love I Festival (Adina Edwards)
8. Feel No Pain (Jackie Brown)
9. Jennie (Jimmy London)
10. Simpleton (The Cordells)

Rel: Nov 1973
RRP: £2.19[1]
        £2.14[4]
Del: 1976[5]

Listed in *The New Records* under Island even though issued via Mooncrest. No tape versions notified to *The New Cassettes & Cartridges* nor *Cassettes & Cartridges*.

The B&C Discography: 1968 to 1975

DRLS 5004 TOOTS AND THE MAYTELS: In the Dark
1. Got To Be There
2. In The Dark
3. Having A Party
4. Time Tough
5. I See You
6. Take a Look In The Mirror

1. Take Me Home Country Roads
2. Fever
3. Love Gonna Walk Out On Me
4. Revolution
5. 54–36
6. Sailing On

Rel: Sep 1974[4]
RRP: £2.25[4]
Del: 1975[5]

Cassette: ZCDRL 5004
8–track: Y8DRL 5004

Rel: Sep 1974[2]
Rel: Sep 1974[2] (del: 1977[5])

RRP: £2.40[2]
RRP: £2.40[2]

DRLS 5005 FREDDIE McKAY: Lonely Man
1. Lonely Man
2. I'm Not Your Love
3. Where Can I Find True Love
4. I'm A Free Man
5. Peace In The Garden

1. If You Should Dream My Life Over
2. Losing Your Love
3. Black Beauty
4. If You Must Go
5. 100 lbs Of Clay

Rel: Feb[1/4]/
Mar 1975[1]
RRP: £2.25[1]

No tape versions notified to *The New Cassettes & Cartridges* nor *Cassettes & Cartridges*.

DRLS 5006 BYRON LEE AND THE DRAGONAIRES: The Midas Touch
1. Up Park Camp
2. None Shall Escape The Judgement
3. Girl We Got A Date
4. You Can't Blame The Youth
5. Here I Am (Come And Take Me)

1. I Shot The Sheriff
2. You Must Believe
3. My Girl
4. Road Block
5. Ode To Billy Joe

Rel: Mar[1]/
Apr '75[1/4]
RRP: £2.25

Cassette: ZCDRL 5006
8–track: Y8DRL 5006

Rel: May 1975[2]
Rel: May 1975[2] (del: 1977[5])

RRP: £2.56[2]
RRP: £2.65[2]

DRLS 5007 NO RELEASE

DRLS 5008 HOPETOWN LEWIS: Dynamic Hopetown Lewis
1. Drift Away
2. Pied Piper
3. Keep On Singing
4. Working It Down To The Bone
5. Pick Yourself Up
6. God's Little Children

1. Show Me Some Loving
2. Goodbye Yesterday
3. Leaving Babylon
4. Take My Heart
5. Baby Don't Get Hooked On Me
6. City Of New Orleans

Rel: May[4]/
Jun 1975[1]
RRP: £2.55[1]

No tape versions notified to *The New Cassettes & Cartridges* nor *Cassettes & Cartridges*.

DRA sequence 7" singles

Early singles were released via Island and many – if not all – of these would have had no more than one pressing run, though unsold stock may later have been distributed by Mooncrest. At switchover there must have been a large number of pre–existing 7" label blanks because singles from (most likely) DRA 1013 to (almost certainly) DRA 1026 have Island credits inexpertly blacked out with "Manufactured by Mooncrest Records Ltd" text printed above. Later on new label blanks were printed with "Marketed by B&C Records" in line with other B&C–related labels. So far only DRA 1013 has come to light with original Island credits on some copies and the overprinted Mooncrest credits on others, though it is possible that earlier releases still on catalogue may also have had credits overprinted. All that can be said is that none have come to light during research. The earlier run of Island–era singles are listed, not just for the sake of completeness, but

The B&C Discography: 1968 to 1975

because the majority were still available via Mooncrest and later, following the demise of the original Mooncrest, unsold stock, via the resurrected Trojan – those Island releases later available via Trojan have this noted. Oddly, at least one early release was reissued by Polydor during the Mooncrest era. All singles viewed have 4–prong die–cut centres, except DRA 1024 and DRA 1034, which are confirmed only with solid centres. At least some releases were pressed up with the same track on both sides for promotional use as per B&C practice. In line with other labels, this is not documented in these listings.

Island–era releases

DRA 1001 HOPETOWN LEWIS: City Of New Orleans / The Wind Cries Mary
Rel: 23 Mar 1973[3]
Reissued on Polydor in April 1974[5].

DRA 1002 THE SCORPION WITH THE BORIS GARDINER HAPPENING: Deadly Sting / THE BORIS GARDINER HAPPENING: Boing Boing
Rel: 9 Mar 1973[3]
Later available via the resurrected Trojan label[5].

DRA 1003 KEN PARKER: Will The Circle Be Unbroken / THE DYNAMITES: Will The Circle Be Unbroken (instrumental)
Rel: 9 Mar 1973[3]
Later available via the resurrected Trojan label[5].

DRA 1004 HENRY AND LIZA: Hole Under Cratches / TIVOLIS: Hole Under Cratches (Instrumental)
Rel: 23 Mar 1973[3]
Later available via the resurrected Trojan label[5].

DRA 1005 NO RELEASE

DRA 1006 THE CLARENDONIANS: Walking Up A One Way Street / THE DYNAMITES: Walking Up A One Way Street (Instrumental)
Rel: 13 Apr 1973[3]

DRA 1007 TOOTS AND THE MAYTELS: Sit Right Down / Screwface Underground / Pomps And Pride
Rel: 20 Apr 1973[3]
Two tracks on b–side. Later available via the resurrected Trojan label[5].

DRA 1008 BYRON LEE AND THE DRAGONAIRES: In The Mood / Black On
Rel: 13 Apr 1973[3]
Listed as later available via the resurrected Trojan label[5].

DRA 1009 ADINA EDWARDS: Why Don't You Write Me / Just A Closer Walk With Thee
Rel: 11 May 1973[3]

DRA 1010 JIMMI LONDON: Jennie / I Wonder If I Care As Much
Rel: 11 May 1973[3]
Later available via the resurrected Trojan label[5].

The B&C Discography: 1968 to 1975

DRA 1011 **HOPETOWN LEWIS:** *Groovin' Out On Life / God Bless Whoever Sent You*
Rel: 1 Jun 1973[3]
Later available via the resurrected Trojan label[5].

DRA 1012 **FREDDIE McKAY:** *Our Rendez–Vous / Black Beauty*
Rel: 1 Jun 1973[3]
Later available via the resurrected Trojan label[5].

DRA 1013 **TOOTS AND THE MAYTELS:** *Country Road / Funky Kingston*
Rel: 13 Jul 1973[3]
Copies exist with both original Island credits and with Island credits blocked out and Mooncrest credits added. The release date above represents the original Island release just a month in advance of the switch to Mooncrest. Later available via the resurrected Trojan label[5].

DRA 1014 **STRANGER AND GLADYS:** *Conqueror / Conqueror (Instrumental Version)*
Rel: 13 Jul[3]/Aug 1973[5]
Release originally advised for July, so the August date may represent the repromotion by Mooncrest.

Mooncrest–era releases

DRA 1015 **KEN PARKER:** *Say Wonderful Things / It's True*
Rel: 26 Oct 1973[3]

DRA 1016 **TOOTS AND THE MAYTELS:** *In The Dark / Sailing On*
Rel: 9 Nov[3]/30 Nov 1973[3]

DRA 1017 **ERIC DONALDSON:** *What A Festival / Version Festival*
Rel: 9 Nov 1973[3]

DRA 1018 **ERIC DONALDSON:** *The Way You Do The Things You Do / Version*
Rel: 16 Nov 1973[3]

DRA 1019 **JIMMY LONDON:** *No Letter Today / The Road Is Rough*
Rel: 29 Mar 1974[3]
Credited here as "Jimmy" (with a "y"). Later available via the resurrected Trojan label[5].

DRA 1020 **ERIC DONALDSON:** *Watch What You Are Doing To Me / You Must Believe*
Rel: 29 Mar 1974[3]

DRA 1021 **MAYTELS:** *Fever / It Was Written Down*
Rel: 5 Apr 1974[8]

DRA 1022 **FREDDIE McKAY:** *Dream My Life Over / YOUTH STARS: Version*
Rel: 19 Apr 1974[3]

DRA 1023 **ERIC DONALDSON:** *Beautiful Maiden / THE DYNAMITES: Version*
Rel: 28 Jun 1974[3]

DRA 1024 **THE MAYTELS:** *Time Tough / Version*
Rel: not notified to *The New Singles*
Only solid centred copies confirmed.

The B&C Discography: 1968 to 1975

DRA 1025   *TINGA STEWART: The Message / Dub*
Rel: not notified to *The New Singles*

DRA 1026   *TOOTS AND THE MAYTELS: Sailing On / If You Act This Way*
Rel: 15 Nov 1974[3]
This is the last confirmed release on overprinted Island label blanks.

DRA 1027   *ERIC DONALDSON: A Weh We A Go Do / SOUL DEFENDERS: A Weh We A Go Do (Part 2)*
Rel: 15 Nov 1974[3]
Confirmed as the joint first release, along with DRA 1028, with the amended "Marketed by B&C" credit on labels. Somehow, DRA 1029, released the same day, slipped out with no distribution credits.

DRA 1028   *MAX ROMEO: No Joshua No / Instrumental*
Rel: 15 Nov 1974[3]

DRA 1029   *THE JAMAICANS: My Heart Just Keeps On Breaking / My Heart Just Keeps On Breaking (Instrumental)*
Rel: 15 Nov 1974[3]
No distribution credits on labels.

DRA 1030   *NORRIS WEIR: Reggay Revolution / Reggay Revolution II*
Rel: 22 Nov 1974[3]
Only solid centred copies confirmed.

DRA 1031   *TELLERS: A–Ya–It–Deh / ENGINEERS: A–Hit–Dub*
Rel: 22 Nov 1974[3]

DRA 1032   *THE ETHIOPIANS: Knowledge Is Power / Power Version*
Rel: 14 Feb 1975[3] (del: 1977[5])

DRA 1033   *BOBBY ELLIS: Up Park Camp / Verse 4*
Rel: 14 Feb 1975[3] (del: 1977[5])

DRA 1034   *ROBERTA SWEED: Words (Are Impossible) / THE DYNAMITES: Words (Are Impossible)*
Rel: 14 Mar 1975[3]
Only solid centred copies confirmed.

Sussex

The majority of LPs on Sussex were back catalogue from the US Sussex label and were issued in November 1974. Most had previously been available in the UK via A&M and, despite supposed deletion, these were still freely available for many years, which must have confused the issue. Sussex received a bit of a 'double whammy' in 1975 with both B&C's liquidation and the shutting down of the US Sussex label for non–payment of tax. Most releases were therefore deleted in 1975. A few LPs were listed as still available until 1976 with some singles and tape versions of albums listed as 1977 deletions (and one or two listed as still on catalogue as at 1979). These would most likely have represented original unsold stock and were, by that time, distributed via the resurrected Trojan label.

LPSX sequence LPs

LPSX 1   BILL WITHERS: Still Bill

1. Lonely Town, Lonely Street
2. Let Me In Your Life
3. Who Is He (And What Is He to You)?
4. Use Me
5. Lean On Me

1. Kissing My Love
2. I Don't Know
3. Another Day To Run
4. I Don't Want You On My Mind
5. Take It All In And Check It All Out

Rel: Nov 1974[1/4]
RRP: £2.45[1]
Del: 1975[5]

No tape versions notified to *The New Cassettes & Cartridges* nor *Cassettes & Cartridges*.

LPSX 2   BILL WITHERS: +'Justments

1. You
2. The Same Love That Made Me Laugh
3. Stories
4. Green Grass
5. Ruby Lee

1. Heartbreak Road
2. Can We Pretend
3. Liza
4. Make A Smile For Me
5. Railroad Man

Rel: Nov 1974[1/4]
RRP: £2.45[1]
Del: 1975[5]

Cassette: ZCSUS 2
8–track: Y8SUS 2

Rel: Dec 1974[2]
Rel: Dec 1974[2] (del: 1977[5])

RRP: £2.65[2]
RRP: £2.65[2]

LPSX 3   BILL WITHERS: Just As I Am

1. Harlem
2. Ain't No Sunshine
3. Grandma's Hands
4. Sweet Wanomi
5. Everybody's Talkin'
6. Do It Good

1. Hope She'll Be Happier
2. Let It Be
3. I'm Her Daddy
4. In My Heart
5. Moanin' And Groanin'
6. Better Off Dead

Rel: Nov 1974[1/4]
RRP: £2.45[1]
Del: 1975[5]

No tape versions notified to *The New Cassettes & Cartridges* nor *Cassettes & Cartridges*.

LPSX 4   THE SOUL SEARCHERS: Salt Of The Earth

1. I Rolled It You Hold It
2. Blow Your Whistle
3. Close To You
4. Funk To The Folks

1. Ain't It Heavy
2. Windsong
3. Ashley's Roachclip
4. We Share
5. If It Ain't Funky

Rel: Nov 1974[1/4]
RRP: £2.45[1]
Del: 1975[5]

Cassette: ZCSUS 4
8–track: Y8SUS 4

Rel: Dec 1974[2]
Rel: Dec 1974[2] (del: 1977[5])

RRP: £2.65[2]
RRP: £2.65[2]

The B&C Discography: 1968 to 1975

LPSX 5   MASTERFLEET: High On The Sea
1. First Voyage
2. Skull Stone (To The Bone)
3. Let Love Stand
4. Man And Child
5. Well Phase I

1. Malfunction
2. Academy Awards
3. When You're A New Born
4. Until Tomorrow
5. Well Phase II

Rel: Nov 1974[1/4]
RRP: £2.45[1]

No tape versions notified to *The New Cassettes & Cartridges* nor *Cassettes & Cartridges*.

LPSX 6   CREATIVE SOURCE: Creative Force
1. You Can't Hide Love
2. Let Me In Your Life
3. Lovesville
4. You're Too Good To Be True
5. Wild Flower

1. Magic Carpet Ride
2. Who Is He And What Is He To You
3. Oh Love

Rel: Nov 1974[1/4]
RRP: £2.45[1]
Del: 1976[5]

Cassette: ZCSUS 6
8-track: Y8SUS 6

Rel: Dec 1974[2] (del: 1977[5])
Rel: Dec 1974[2]

RRP: £2.65[2]
RRP: £2.65[2]

LPSX 7   CREATIVE SOURCE: Migration
1. I'm Gonna Get There
2. Harlem
3. I Just Can't See Myself Without You

1. Keep On Movin'
2. Migration
3. Corazon
4. Let Me Be The One

Rel: Nov 1974[1/4]
RRP: £2.45[1]
Del: 1976[5]

Cassette: ZCSUS 7
8-track: Y8SUS 7

Rel: Feb 1975[2] (del: 1977[5])
Rel: Feb 1975[2]

RRP: £2.65[2]
RRP: £2.65[2]

LPSX 8   LONETTE McKEE: Lonette
1. Message From The Earth
2. You Mean A Lot To Me
3. Save It (Don't Give It Away)
4. I'm Alone
5. Lay Me Down Easy

1. Love Won't Come Easy
2. Do To Me
3. See Ourselves, Be Ourselves, Free Ourselves
4. The Way I Want To Touch You
5. To Whom It May Concern

Rel: Feb 1975[4]
RRP: unknown

Cassette: ZCSUS 8
8-track: Y8SUS 8

Rel: Mar 1975[2] (del: 1977[5])
Rel: Mar 1975[2] (del: 1977[5])

RRP: £2.65[2]
RRP: £2.65[2]

LPSX 9   DENNIS COFFEY: Instant Coffee
1. Sonata
2. Moon Star
3. Theme From Enter The Dragon

1. Chicano
2. A Time For Love
3. Kathy
4. Outrageous (The Mind Excursion)

Rel: Apr 1975[1]
RRP: £2.25[1]

No tape versions notified to *The New Cassettes & Cartridges* nor *Cassettes & Cartridges*.

LPSX 10   BILL WITHERS: The Best Of Bill Withers
1. Lean On Me
2. Grandma's Hands
3. Harlem
4. Use Me
5. Everybody's Talkin'

1. Ain't No Sunshine
2. Kissing My Love
3. You
4. The Same Love That Made Me Laugh
5. Who Is He (And What Is He To You)

Rel: Apr 1975[1/4]
RRP: £2.25[1]
Del: 1975[5]

Cassette: ZCSUS 10
8-track: Y8SUS 10

Rel: May 1975[2]
Rel: May 1975[2] (del: 1977[5])

RRP: £2.65[2]
RRP: £2.65[2]

The B&C Discography: 1968 to 1975

LPDX sequence double LP

LPDX 101 **BILL WITHERS:** *"Live" At Carnegie Hall*

Record 1, side 1
1. Use One
2. Friend Of Mine
3. Ain't No Sunshine
4. Grandma's Hands (With Rap)

Record 1, side 2
1. World Keeps Going Around
2. Let Me In Your Life (With Rap)
3. Better Off Dead
4. For My Friend

Rel: Nov 1974[1/4]
RRP: £2.45[1]
Del: 1975[5]

Record 2, side 1
1. Can't Write Left Handed
2. Lean On Me
3. Lonely Town Lonely Street
4. Hope She'll Be Happier

Record 2, side 2
1. Let Us Love
2. Harlem/Cold Baloney

The RRP in *The New Records* is probably wrong. More likely, this was around £3.49. No tape versions notified to *The New Cassettes & Cartridges* nor *Cassettes & Cartridges*.

SSX sequence 7" singles

SSX 1 **CREATIVE SOURCE:** *Who Is He And What Is He To You (Vocal) / Who Is He And What Is He To You (Instrumental)*
Rel: 27 Sep 1974[3]

SSX 2 **SOUL SEARCHERS:** *Blow Your Whistle / Funk To The Folks*
Rel: 4 Oct 1974[3]

SSX 3 **MASTER FLEET:** *Well Phase I / Well Phase II*
Rel: 4 Oct 1974[3]

SSX 4 **LONETTE McKEE:** *Save It (Don't Give It Away) / Do To Me*
Rel: not notified to *The New Singles*
Also rumoured to exist with b-side titled "Do It To Me", though this is unconfirmed.

SSX 5 **CREATIVE SOURCE:** *Migration / Keep On Movin'*
Rel: 3 Jan 1975[3] (del: 1977[5])

SSX 6 **DENNIS COFFEE:** *Getting It On '75 / Chicano*
Rel: 24 Jan 1975[3] (del: 1977[5])

SSX 7 **BILL WITHERS:** *Heartbreak Road / Ruby Lee*
Rel: 7 Feb 1975[3]

SSX 8 **GALLERY:** *I Belive In Music / Louisina Line*
Rel: 4 Apr 1975[3] (del: 1977[5])

SSX 9 **BILL WITHERS:** *Lean On Me / Use Me*
Rel: 11 Apr 1975[3]

Seven Sun

A bit of a sad one, this. The Seven Sun label was originally distributed by President Records and released thirteen singles and at least one (extremely valuable) LP between February 1972 and September 1974. There was a hiatus during which distribution switched to B&C. At least two of the first three B&C releases were scheduled for late June 1975 release, just in time to be swallowed up in B&C's liquidation. All copies viewed have a very large "A" printed on the a–side – does this denote that they are promotional copies? Or was this just to give a big hint as to which side they wanted deejays to play? If the former, perhaps no normal stock copies were ever pressed. Does anyone know?

SSUN sequence 7" singles

SSUN 14   *NORMAN BEATON: Love Is Around / The Skin*
Rel: 20 Jun 1975[3]

SSUN 15   *100% PROOF: Kisses Kisses Kisses / He's The Guy*
Rel: 20 Jun 1975[3]

SSUN 16   *BLACK VELVET: I'm On My Way / Groove Along*
Rel: not notified to *The New Singles*

And Finally...

To be strictly accurate, the Seven Sun label came last, datewise, but at least the existence of copies of all three B&C–era singles on that label are confirmed (whether they got as far as the shops or not is another matter), whereas copies of neither cassette nor 8–track of this album have come to light, though this doesn't mean that it doesn't exist.

Anyway, to the album. It's April 1975 and it is obvious that the ship is sinking. What to do? How about putting out a special, cross–label greatest hits package. Okay, but just what audience is this particular selection aimed at? Ronco and K–tel album buyers by the look of it – all it does is to pull together the B&C Group's highest–charting hits, but with no real attempt at consistency of style – moving from hard rock to rock steady to singalong folk pop to progressive rock to soul – and that's just the first six tracks.

As already mentioned, whether this got as far as the shops is unknown, but it was advised to both Francis Antony and *Music Master* – it was listed in the May 1975 edition of *The New Cassettes & Cartridges* as a B&C label release – but adverts in the music press seem to be conspicuous by their absence. On the other hand, there are deletion dates for both tape formats in *Music Master*, which lists the distributor as the resurrected Trojan. This does not necessarily mean that the album existed in any form other than on paper – as with Moon 51, this might just represent the point at which Trojan got fed up with being asked for something that didn't exist and formally deleted it.

Lots of B&C labels are represented here: Mooncrest – Nazareth and Hotshots; Charisma – Rare Bird, Lindisfarne, Genesis, Gary Shearston and The Nice; People – Don Downing; B&C – Atomic Rooster; Trojan – Jimmy Cliff, Greyhound, John Holt and Ken Boothe; Harry J – Bob and Marcia; Horse – Scott English. The Desmond Dekker and the Aces track was a hit on Pyramid, distributed at that point by Doctor Bird, but the label later became part of the B&C Group. The Bill Withers track was a hit on A&M, but the track was currently licensed to B&C via the Sussex label. There was also a bit of cheating going on with The Nice track because this was not the hit version, but was a live version. Well, okay, the live version was from a top ten LP, if you want to be pedantic, but the hit single it certainly wasn't!

A last–ditch cross–label tape–only hits package

ZCB 551/Y8BC 551   *VARIOUS: High Powered Hits*

1. Broken Down Angel (Nazareth)
2. Isrealites (Desmond Dekker)
3. Lady Eleanor (Lindisfarne)
4. I Know What I Like (Genesis)
5. Black And White (Greyhound)
6. Lean On Me (Bill Withers)
7. Wonderful World, Beautiful People
   (Jimmy Cliff)
8. Young, Gifted And Black
   (Bob And Marcia)
9. I Get A Kick Out Of You
   (Gary Shearston)
10. Gaye (Clifford T. Ward)

1. Meet Me On The
   Corner (Lindisfarne)
2. Sympathy (Rare Bird)
3. Help Me Make It Through The Night
   (John Holt)
4. Lonely Days Lonely Nights
   (Don Downing)
5. America (The Nice)
6. Tomorrow Night (Atomic Rooster)
7. Snoopy Vs. The Red Baron (Hotshots)
8. This Flight Tonight (Nazareth)
9. Brandy (Scott Englilsh)
10. Everything I Own (Ken Boothe)

Rel: May 1975[2]
RRP: £2.65[2]
Del: 1977[5]

It is the purest guesswork that there were ten tracks on each side. *America* would almost certainly have been an edited version, possibly as per later issue on Charisma's *Repeat Performance* LP.

The B&C Discography: 1968 to 1975

Other titles that you are bound to like!

Find out more about these and other books from:
www.bristol–folk.co.uk and/or www.lulu.com/spotlight/vinylattic

Transacord: Sounds of Steam – with free CD

The Famous Charisma Discography

The Saydisc & Village Thing Discography

Bristol Folk: a discographical history

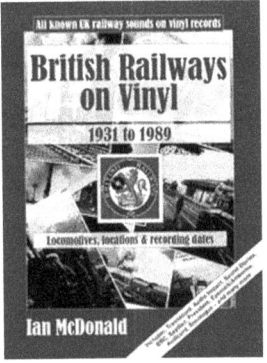
British Railways on Vinyl: Ian McDonald's magnum opus

The Virgin Discography The 1970s

...and for those that want to document their entire record collection, what you need is a database...

www.ingramcontent.com/pod-product-compliance
Lightning Source LLC
Chambersburg PA
CBHW060915190426
43197CB00012BA/2474